Depth Perception
Through Motion

**ACADEMIC PRESS
SERIES IN COGNITION AND PERCEPTION**

SERIES EDITORS:
Edward C. Carterette
Morton P. Friedman
Department of Psychology
University of California, Los Angeles
Los Angeles, California

DEPTH PERCEPTION THROUGH MOTION

WITHDRAWN

Myron L. Braunstein

School of Social Sciences
University of California
Irvine, California

ACADEMIC PRESS   New York   San Francisco   London

A Subsidiary of Harcourt Brace Jovanovich, Publishers

ACADEMIC PRESS, INC.
111 Fifth Avenue, New York, New York 10003

United Kingdom Edition published by
ACADEMIC PRESS, INC. (LONDON) LTD.
24/28 Oval Road, London NW1

Library of Congress Cataloging in Publication Data

Braunstein, Myron L
    Depth perception through motion.

    (Academic Press series in cognition and perception)
    Bibliography: p.
    1.   Depth perception.   2.   Movement, Psychology of.
I.   Title.
BF469.B7   153.7'52   75-26344
ISBN 0-12-127950-2

Contents

Preface

The visual world is a three-dimensional world. It is also a world of motion. The human observer is often in motion; the eye is always in motion; and other people, animals, and objects may be moving with respect to the observer. To what extent does motion determine the perception of depth? This is a question that has generated increasing interest among researchers in visual perception in recent years. There is now a considerable body of research, and it seems appropriate to bring this research together in a book dedicated to this topic.

The book is intended for researchers and graduate students interested in depth perception in dynamic environments. Although it is primarily for those specializing in visual perception, it should also be of interest to specialists in other fields, ranging from kinetic art to human factors engineering. For this reason, introductory material on depth perception has been included in the first chapter, and assumptions of specialized knowledge have generally been avoided.

Chapter 1 discusses the origins of the study of depth perception in philosophy and describes the cue and gradient concepts. A short chapter on early discoveries of the perception of depth through motion follows. Chapter 3 describes the geometrical considerations required for the study of depth perception in dynamic environments, relying on graphic rather than mathematical demonstrations of these considerations. (Some of the relevant equations are presented in the Appendix.) The next three chapters consider the current state of knowledge with respect to three major research problems in this area: dynamic factors leading to the perception of depth, slant judgments in dynamic displays, and factors affecting the accuracy of perceived direction of rotary motion. The final chapter presents a theoretical approach in which perception is related to other forms of human problem solving, and perceptual processes are regarded as heuristic processes. An appendix on computer animation is provided for the researcher who would like to produce stimulus materials of the type described in this book, with a minimum of specialized equipment.

I would like to express my appreciation to John W. Payne, who collaborated with me in many of the experimental investigations cited in this book, participated in numerous discussions on the direction that this book was to take, and critically reviewed earlier drafts of the manuscript. This book would not exist in its present form without his important contributions. I would also like to thank Alice B. Macy for assisting in the preparation of the manuscript, Mark W. Vernoy for reviewing portions of the manuscript and designing the computer-generated figures, Karen P. Jablonski and Kenneth R. Stern for assisting in the preparation of the bibliography, and Wayne Deeter for assisting in the development of the graphics software package described in the Appendix. The illustrations include original drawings by Greg Pautsch and original photographs by Thom Batey and by Dean Pautsch. I am grateful for the research support which I have received from the National Science Foundation Program in Psychobiology. All of my publications in this area since 1966 were prepared with National Science Foundation support.

Acknowledgments

FIGURE 1.1 From: Wald, G. Eye and camera. *Scientific American,* August 1950, *183*, 32–41. Copyright © 1950 by Scientific American, Inc. All rights reserved.

FIGURE 1.5. From *The World Book Encyclopedia.* © 1974 Field Enterprises Educational Corporation.

FIGURE 2.2. From: Miles, W. R. Movement interpretations of the silhouette of a revolving fan. *American Journal of Psychology,* 1931, *43*, 392–405. Fig. 1.

FIGURE 2.7. From: Metzger, W. *Gesetze der Sehens.* Frankfurt am Main: Waldemar Kramer, 1953. Fig. 380.

FIGURE 2.8. Designs by Fred Duncan; Copyright by Research Media, Inc.

FIGURES 3.1, 3.2, AND 3.3. From: Gibson, J. J. *The senses considered as perceptual systems.* Boston: Houghton Mifflin, 1966. Figs. 10.4, 10.5 and 10.6. Copyright 1966. By permission of Houghton Mifflin Company.

FIGURES 4.1, 4.2, AND 4.5. From: Wallach, H., & O'Connell, D. N. The kinetic depth effect. *Journal of Experimental Psychology,* 1953, *45* 205–217.

Figs. 1, 2, 3, and 4. Copyright 1953 by the American Psychological Association. Reprinted by permission.

FIGURE 4.7. From: White, B. J., & Mueser, G. E. Accuracy in reconstructing the arrangement of elements generating kinetic depth displays. *Journal of Experimental Psychology*, 1960, 60, 1–11. Figs. 1 and 2. Copyright 1960 by the American Psychological Association. Reprinted by permission.

FIGURE 4.11. From: Braunstein, M. L. Sensitivity of the observer to transformations of the visual field. *Journal of Experimental Psychology*, 1966, 72, 683–689. Fig. 1. Copyright 1966 by the American Psychological Association. Reprinted by permission.

FIGURES 4.12, 4.14, AND 4.15. From: Braunstein, M. L. Depth perception in rotating dot patterns: Effects of numerosity and perspective. *Journal of Experimental Psychology*, 1962, 64, 415–420. Figs. 1, 2, and 3. Copyright 1962 by the American Psychological Association. Reprinted by permission.

FIGURE 4.16. From Börjesson, E., & Von Hofsten, C. Spatial determinants of depth perception in two-dot motion patterns. *Perception and Psychophysics*, 1972, 11, 263–268. Figs. 2, 4, 5, and 6.

FIGURE 4.17. From: Börjesson, E., & Von Hofsten, C. Visual perception of motion in depth: Application of a factor model to three-dot motion patterns. *Perception and Psychophysics*, 1973, 13, 169–179. Figs. 2, 3, and 5.

FIGURE 4.18 AND 4.19 From: Wallach, H., Weisz, A., & Adams, P. A. Circles and derived figures in rotation. *American Journal of Psychology*, 1956, 69, 48–59. Figs. 6, 8, and 9.

FIGURE 4.20. From: Fischer, G. J. Factors affecting estimation of depth with variations of the stereokinetic effect. *American Journal of Psychology*, 1956, 69, 252–257. Fig. 1.

FIGURE 4.21. From: Gibson, E. J., Gibson, J. J., Smith, O. W., & Flock, H. Motion parallax as a determinant of perceived depth. *Journal of Experimental Psychology*, 1959, 58, 40–51. Figs. 1 and 3. Copyright 1959 by the American Psychological Association. Reprinted by permission.

FIGURE 5.2. From: Gibson, J. J. The perception of visual surfaces. *American Journal of Psychology*, 1950, 63, 367–384. Fig. 2.

FIGURE 5.3. Reprinted with permission of author and publisher: Flock, H. R., & Moscatelli, A. Variables of surface texture and accuracy of space perceptions. *Perceptual and Motor Skills*, 1964, 19, 327–334. Fig. 1.

FIGURE 5.4. From: Phillips, R. J. Stationary visual texture and the estimation of slant angle. *Quarterly Journal of Experimental Psychology*, 1970, 22, 389–397. Fig. 1.

FIGURE 5.5 From: Attneave, F., & Olson, R. K. Inferences about visual mechanisms from monocular depth effects. *Psychonomic Science*, 1966, 4, 133–134. Fig. 1. .

FIGURE 5.7. From: Clark, W. C., Smith, A. H., & Rabe, A. The interaction of surface texture, outline gradient, and ground in the perception of slant. *Canadian Journal of Psychology*, 1956, *10*, 1–8. Fig. 1.

FIGURE 5.9. From: Braunstein, M. L., & Payne, J. W. Perspective and form ratio as determinants of relative slant judgments. *Journal of Experimental Psychology*, 1969, *81*, 584–590. Fig. 2.Copyright 1969 by the American Psychological Association. Reprinted by permission.

FIGURE 6.1. From: Ames, A. Visual perception and the rotating trapezoidal window. *Psychological Monographs*, 1951, *67*(7, Whole No. 324). Fig. 7. Copyright 1951 by the American Psychological Association. Reprinted by permission.

FIGURES 6.3, 6.7, 6.8, AND 6.9; TABLE 6.1: From: Braunstein, M. L. Perception of rotation in depth: A process model. *Psychological Review*, 1972, *79*, 510–524. Figs. 1, 4, 5, and 6; Table 1. Copyright 1972 by the American Psychological Association. Reprinted by permission.

FIGURE 6.4. From: Braunstein, M. L. Perception of rotation in figures with rectangular and trapezoidal features. *Journal of Experimental Psychology*, 1971, *91*, 25–29. Fig. 1. Copyright 1971 by the American Psychological Association. Reprinted by permission.

FIGURE 6.5. From: Börjesson, E. Properties of changing patterns evoking visually perceived oscillation. *Perception and Psychophysics*, 1971, *9*, 303–308. Fig. 1.

Portions of Chapter 6 previously appeared in Braunstein, M. L. Perception of rotation in depth: A process model. *Psychological Review*, 1972, *79*, 510–524. Copyright 1972 by the American Psychological Association. Reprinted by permission.

1

The Paradox of
Depth Perception

HE STUDY OF VISUAL PERCEPTION has easily traceable roots in the
writings of philosophers of the seventeenth and early eighteenth
centuries. These beginnings have had a considerable influence on
modern research and theory, particularly in the study of depth perception.
Attempting to explain three-dimensional perception as the addition of
cues to a two-dimensional retinal image clearly derives from these early
ideas. The conceptualization of motion perception as the linking together
of discrete momentary images is a by-product of these ideas. We will
therefore begin our consideration of the role of motion in depth perception by examining the origins of the ideas that underlie the current
body of knowledge and theory in this area.

1

The Eye–Camera Analogy

The single most influential idea in the history of visual perception was probably the analogy of the eye to the camera. Figure 1.1 illustrates this analogy. Light enters the eye through an adjustable iris just as it enters the camera through a diaphragm, which is usually adjustable. The light is focused by a lens. In the eye, the lens changes its shape as it accommodates to variations in the distances of observed objects. Focusing in

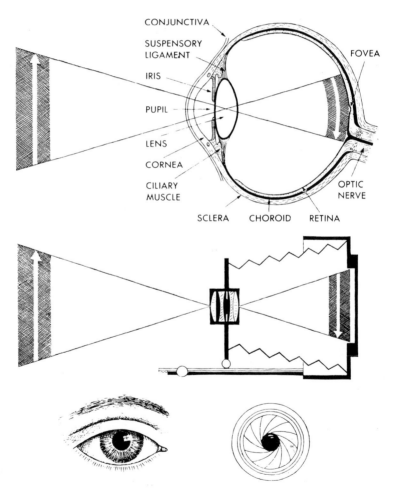

FIGURE 1.1. The eye–camera analogy. [From Wald, G., Eye and camera. *Scientific American*, August 1950, *183*, 32–41. Copyright © 1950 by Scientific American, Inc. All rights reserved.]

the camera is accomplished by varying the distance between the lens and the film. At the back of the eye, the focused light impinges on a layer of photosensitive material in the cells of the retina. This is, to a degree, comparable to the exposure of the photosensitive layer of film to light entering the camera. To this point, the analogy between the eye and the camera is a useful tool for helping people familiar with photography to understand the gross anatomy of the input device of the visual system. There is, however, a hazard in analogies. An analogy may exert an influence on our thinking about a behavioral process that exceeds its original intent and goes beyond its accepted validity. This has occurred with the eye–camera analogy. Rather than limiting its influence to a consideration of the function of parts of the eye in bringing light to the photosensitive pigments in the retina, the analogy has resulted in thinking of visual perception as beginning with a picture of the external world, like the picture taken by a camera. Before we consider the consequences of this influence on the study of visual perception, it will be useful to look at the original form of the eye–camera analogy.

THE CAMERA OBSCURA

The original analogy was not between the eye and the photographic camera. It is much older than that. The camera to which the eye was compared was the camera obscura. The construction of a camera obscura was described by Porta in 1589. All of the windows in a room must be shut and all holes covered except for one a hand's breadth and length. A thin sheet of metal is placed against that hole and a much smaller hole, the size of the little finger, is made in the metal. White paper or clothing is placed on the wall opposite this hole. The outside scene is visible on this wall, although the image is inverted and reverted. This is the basic camera obscura. Porta describes two refinements of the camera: inserting a lens near the small hole to make the images clearer, and inserting a second lens so that the images are no longer inverted or reverted. He then presents the analogy of the eye to the camera: "The image is let in by the pupil, as by the hole of a window; and that part of the sphere that is set in the middle of the eye, stands instead of a crystal table [lens] [p. 365]." The camera obscura described by Porta is illustrated in Figure 1.2. A modern version of the device can be seen in Santa Monica, California, where it is a tourist attraction (Figure 1.3).

The analogy of the eye to the camera obscura, like that of the eye to the photographic camera, can be instructive in describing the functions of parts of the eye. The pupil admits light into a dark chamber in the eye, as does the aperture in the camera obscura. The camera obscura may,

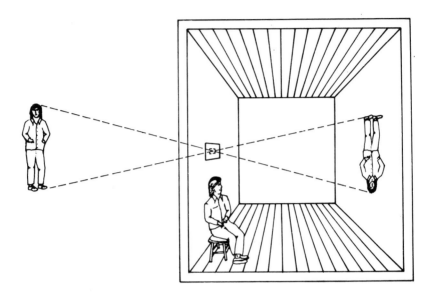

FIGURE 1.2.   The camera obscura.

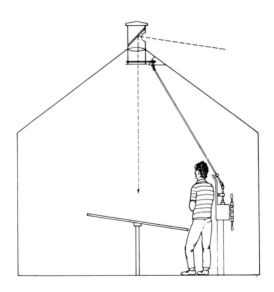

FIGURE 1.3.   The camera obscura at Santa Monica, California. A view of the surrounding area is projected onto the white circular table at the center. The view can be changed by turning the wheel at the right, which rotates the turret 360°.

like the eye, contain a lens which focuses the light. An image is projected onto a surface opposite the lens in the eye, just as in the camera obscura. When the analogy is carried one step further, however, it can present serious difficulties for the perceptual theorist. The next step in a description of the camera obscura is that there is an observer, usually inside the camera, who looks at the image projected on the surface opposite the lens and draws inferences about the external objects responsible for the image.

The Homunculus Problem

What, in the visual system, is the analog of the human observer found within the camera obscura? Many early writers attempting to explain human vision considered this problem.[1] Kepler (1604) leaves to the natural philosopher the question of whether the retinal image "is made to appear before the soul or tribunal of the faculty of vision by a spirit within the cerebral cavities, or the faculty of vision, like a magistrate sent by the soul, goes out from the council chamber of the brain to meet this image in the optic nerves and retina, as if it were descending to a lower court." This question assumes that there is an image apprehended by the faculty of vision. The issue left to be resolved is the locus of the apprehension of the image, at the eye or in the brain. Molyneux (1692) went a step further, placing the problem not only beyond the scope of the science of optics but beyond the bounds of human inquiry. Molyneux states that the retinal image is "perceived by the *sensitive Soul* (whatever it be) the manner of whose Actions and Passions, He only knows who Created and Preserves it, *Whose Ways are Past finding out, and by us unsearchable.*"

In the more modern versions of the eye–camera analogy, which substitute the photographic camera for the camera obscura, the suggestion remains that light entering the eye produces a picture on the retina which, like the picture taken by the camera, is somehow perceived. The implication that there is a homunculus in the visual system that perceives the picture on the retina is less obvious when the photographic camera is used in the analogy, for the functions of taking a picture and looking at a picture are separate with this type of camera. The homunculus implication remains, however, so long as visual perception is thought of as beginning with the formation of a picture that must be apprehended and interpreted.

[1] See Pastore (1971) for a more extensive discussion of the early theories of visual perception.

The use of the photographic camera in the eye–camera analogy, rather than eliminating the homunculus problem, introduces a new difficulty for the perceptual theorist. If this form of the analogy is accepted too literally, perception may be thought of as a series of snapshots rather than as a continuous, dynamic process. Continuous transformations are not directly perceived, according to this concept of visual perception. The observer becomes aware that motion has taken place by comparing his present momentary view of the visual world to a memory trace of a previous view. Transformations must be reconstructed from a sequence of memory traces. The point that continuous transformations are themselves stimuli for visual perception is a relatively recent one, made by Gibson (Gibson, 1950b, 1957; Gibson & Gibson, 1957) over the objection of other theorists (Wallach & O'Connell, 1953) who preferred the memory trace approach. The unfortunate implications of the snapshot analogy might suggest that a motion picture camera should be substituted for the still camera in the eye–camera analogy illustrated in Figure 1.1, but this substitution of a more sophisticated camera does little to eliminate the tendency to regard perception as beginning with a series of still pictures. A motion picture is, after all, a series of snapshots shown in rapid succession.

Updating the Analogy

The tendency to keep the eye–camera analogy alive by substituting more sophisticated cameras for the camera obscura or for the simple photographic camera has not been fully resisted even by those who have most carefully avoided the pitfalls of the analogy. Gibson (1966) has repeatedly called attention to the misleading nature of the eye–camera analogy, yet he states that the eye "is a self-focusing, self-setting, and self-orienting camera whose image becomes optimal because the system compensates for blur, for extremes of illumination, and for being aimed at something uninteresting [p. 33]."

The advent of television has introduced still another version of the analogy and, at least in one dramatic instance, has reintroduced the explicit homunculus. There is a film[2] distributed for use at the high school level in which a narrator explains the functioning of the visual system to a layman, using an animated representation of the internal processes of someone named Joe. There is, first of all, a homunculus inside the eye who supervises the transmission of the retinal image to the brain in the form of electrical impulses. The narrator explains, "The electrical impulses

[2] "Gateways to the Mind," distributed by the Bell System.

come alive as pictures on what we call the master receiver." This appears in the animated portion of the film as a large television screen inside the brain. There is another, larger homunculus observing this screen who responds to the information in the picture by operating various switches on a control panel. The layman in the film asks, as we might have asked the early proponents of the visual spirit concept in perception, "Who's the little man?" The narrator responds, "He represents the thinking part of Joe's brain." This may appear to be an exceedingly naive explanation of vision, produced for use at an introductory level, but it is an especially graphic example of where the eye–camera analogy leads. (The analogy between the eye and a motion picture camera is presented in that film.) If we think of perception as a function performed by a perceiver in the brain, we must next inquire into the perceptual capabilities of that perceiver. The perceiver in the brain, as it engages in perception, must contain still another perceiver. This line of reasoning, of course, could have no conclusion. An alternative would be to ascribe spiritual qualities to the internal perceiver, rendering this perceiver beyond the realm of scientific inquiry. This solution is of little help to the perceptual theorist.

Other Problems with the Analogy

The Inverted Image Problem

Identification of the little man has not been the only difficulty with the analogy. Philosophers and early psychologists who conceived of perception as the interpretation of a two-dimensional picture on the retina believed it necessary to account for the correspondence of perception to the external, physically measurable environment. One dramatic difference between the physical world and the retinal image is that the image is upside down. As shown in Figure 1.4, the tops of objects project onto the bottom of the retina and vice versa. The recognition of this characteristic of the retinal image dates back to the eye–camera analogy. Porta (1558) notes the upside-down appearance of objects viewed in the camera obscura, particularly of the projections of people walking in the street. He corrected this problem by inserting a second lens in the camera to reverse the image again, producing an upright projection. The opinion that perception should correspond to the retinal image was so strongly held by some early scientists that it was suggested that the eye, too, must have a second lens so that the retinal image would be upright. This was, of course, not confirmed as knowledge of the anatomy of the eye increased.

For Molyneux (1692), the inverted image presented no problem. The

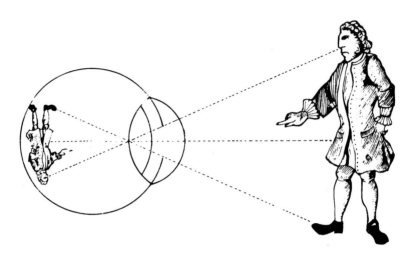

FIGURE 1.4.   Inversion of the retinal image (after Voltaire, 1738).

soul used the eye as an instrument for forming a picture. So long as such a picture was available in the eye, it should not matter which part of the eye contained which part of the picture. The visive faculty was concerned with up and down in the external world and took no notice of up and down in the eye. For the empiricist philosophers there was another solution to the inverted image problem: experience. As we reach for objects we learn that we must reach upward for those that project images at the bottoms of our eyes and downward for those that project images at the tops of our eyes. This implies that up and down within the eye is initially noticed, and we learn to live with the inversion of the retinal image. Variations of this explanation, by Locke (1694), Berkeley (·1709) and others, have greatly influenced experimental psychology. The inverted image issue has given rise to an area of research, perceptual adaptation, that is active and widespread today.

The classic research in perceptual adaptation was reported by Stratton in 1896. Stratton was concerned with evaluating two theories that held the inversion of the retinal image to be necessary for the perception of objects as upright. According to the first theory, objects are projected back into space in the directions in which the rays of light fall upon the retina. The second theory holds that perception of upper or lower in the visual field depends on whether upward or downward eye movements are required to bring objects into focus. According to Stratton, both of these theories require that the retinal image be inverted in order that things be seen in an upright position. In order to test these theories, he developed an optical device that reinverted the image and wore this device for varying periods of time (Stratton, 1896, 1897a, b). He was able to adapt to the "upright" retinal image, at least to a degree. Stratton (1896) used this adaptation as evidence against theories that hold that an inverted retinal image is necessary for the perception of an upright world:

> In fact, the difficulty of seeing things upright by means of upright retinal images seems to consist solely in the resistance offered by the long-established previous experience. . . . But a person whose vision had from the very beginning been under the conditions we have in the present experiment artificially produced, could never possibly feel that such visual perceptions were inverted [p. 617].

Perceptual adaptation of many kinds have been studied since Stratton's pioneering efforts. Adaptation to expansion or contraction of the optic array of one or both eyes (Rock, 1965), in one or two dimensions (Ogle, 1950), to separation of the effective focal points of the eyes (Wallach & Karsh, 1963), to partial rotations (Mikaelian & Held, 1964), and to other distortions have been artificially produced. The conclusions of these studies usually follow Stratton's theme: If a subject can adapt to a particular distortion of the optic array(s), his normal perception of that aspect of the undistorted array must have been acquired through experience. These studies have been used as supporting evidence for the empiricist viewpoint in the nativist–empiricist controversy. We will not be directly concerned with that controversy here, but it should be noted that one does not have to accept the empiricist explanation of the perceptual adaptation results. The ability of an adult animal to alter a behavior pattern is not conclusive evidence that this pattern was originally learned. Very simple behaviors which are generally accepted as innately determined can be altered through training. The change in the size of the pupil with changes in the intensity of light at the eye, for example, can be conditioned. The relevant point here is that the inverted image controversy itself need not have occurred. If the retina had been conceived of as an information-gathering device rather than the locus of a picture, the question of relating up and down in the retina to perceived up and down would have been much less significant. We do not, after all, concern ourselves with the relationship between points stimulated in the receptor organs of the ear and the location of sound sources in the external world.

FLATNESS OF THE IMAGE

Inversion of the projected image was not the only major discrepancy between the retinal image and the external world to which attention was drawn by the eye–camera analogy. The projected image in the camera obscura was obviously flat. In fact it was the capability of producing a representation of the three-dimensional world on a flat surface that generated the major application of the camera obscura. This was its use as a drawing aid. The artist who wanted to produce a two-dimensional picture that faithfully represented the geometrical relationships produced at the eye by a three-dimensional scene simply put his canvas inside the camera obscura on the wall opposite the aperture and traced the projected scene. He inserted a second lens if he wished to avoid working with an upside-down picture. This procedure was cumbersome because the artist had to be between the aperture and the canvas where he partially obscured the image he was attempting to trace. This problem was solved through the use of a ground glass screen as the wall opposite the aperture. The artist was then outside the camera. A final refinement was the portable camera obscura, shown in Figure 1.5. This device, invented by Boyle, was widely used in the seventeenth and eighteenth centuries (Encyclopedia Britannica, 1968). The device may have served well those interested in understanding the principles of perspective in drawing; however, it emphasized the flatness and picture-like quality of the projected image in the camera obscura and, by analogy, the flatness of the retinal image.

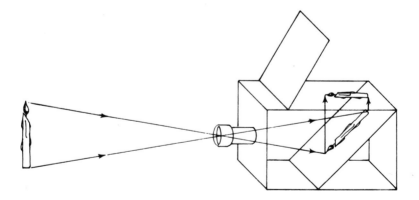

FIGURE 1.5. The portable camera obscura. The external scene (left) projects through a double-convex lens onto a mirror, positioned at a 45° angle inside the camera, and is reflected onto a ground glass screen at the top, where it can be traced by the artist. [From *The World Book Encyclopedia.* © 1974 Field Enterprises Educational Corporation.]

Unlike the inverted image problem, there was no straightforward solution to the flatness of the image. One could not produce a compelling impression of depth merely by adding a second lens, as could be done to eliminate the inversion of a projected image, at least not until the invention of the stereoscope. With the camera obscura serving as a model of the eye, and with the resulting concept of perception beginning with a picture projected onto a flat surface, it was concluded that depth could not be directly perceived. This was the conclusion of Locke and Berkeley, two of the philosophers whose influence on theoretical approaches to visual perception has been greatest. They presumed that the mind apprehended a flat retinal image. Through the association with ideas based on past experiences of simultaneously touching solid objects and observing the retinal images they project, rapid, unconscious judgments were made about the solidity of the objects represented in the flat image. Locke (1694) illustrates this explanation of depth perception in the following passage:

> When we set before our eyes a round globe of any uniform colour, e.g., gold, alabaster, or jet, it is certain that the idea thereby imprinted on our mind is of a flat circle, variously shadowed, with serveral degrees of light and brightness coming to our eyes. But we having, by use, been accustomed to perceive what kind of appearance convex bodies are wont to make in us; what alterations are made in the reflections of light by the difference of the sensible figures of bodies;—judgment presently, by an habitual custom alters the appearances into their causes [p. 186].

The explanation of how the mind accomplishes these judgments is incomplete. Locke's philosophical orientation is dualistic. The mind is considered to be spiritual and its processes are not detailed. This dualism is apparent in the following passage from the same work concerning the conversion of the flat retinal image into judgments of solid objects:

> Nor need we wonder that this is done with so little notice, if we consider how quick the actions of the mind are performed. For, as itself is thought to take up no space, to have no extension; so its actions seem to require no time, but many of them seem to be crowded into an instant. I speak this in comparison to the action of the body [pp. 188–189].

Berkeley (1709) similarly handled the perception of depth on the basis of flat retinal images as an accomplishment of the mind based on past associations between vision and touch. Berkeley also held the mind to be synonymous with the soul or spiritual substance, though he did set forth certain postulates about the functioning of the mind that he used as a basis for rejecting a competing theory of vision. His first postulate was "that when the mind perceives any *idea*, not immediately and of itself, it must be by the means of some other *idea* [p. 15]." To this he added the postulate "that no *idea* which is not itself perceived, can be to me the means of perceiving any other *idea* [p. 15]." He used these postulates to reject the theory that distance is perceived on the basis of the angles between the two optic axes when an object is fixated, and on the decrease in the divergence of rays subtending an object as the distance of the object increases. Using his two postulates, he argues: "In vain shall all the *mathematicians* in the world tell me, that I perceive certain *lines* and *angles* which introduce into my mind the various *ideas* of *distance*; so long as I myself am conscious of no such thing [italics his; pp. 15–16]." In place of the competing geometric theory, Berkeley proposed three means by which distance is indirectly perceived. The perception of distance in each case required the past association of the means with a tangible idea of distance, for Berkeley considered distance to be an idea that could not be directly perceived. The first means was the perception of sensations arising from the disposition of the eyes, or "convergence." (This may seem contradictory as Berkeley rejected the "mathematicians'" use of convergence to explain distance perception. What Berkeley rejected was the use of the geometry of convergence as a direct means of perceiving distance, without the need to associate the sensations of the muscles controlling the direction of the eyes with tangible ideas of distance.) The second means, termed "confusion" by Berkeley, referred to the blurred appearance of an object that is brought very close to the eye. Again, the association between blurred appearance and distance was held to be learned by the association of varying appearances with varying distances perceived by the sense of touch. The third means, "straining," refers to the effort (accommodation or change in shape of the lens) required to bring such a near object into focus. These three means were described by Berkeley as "sensations or ideas" which introduce the idea of distance into the mind.

The two postulates on which Berkeley's theory of vision rests represent another intrusion of the homunculus concept into perceptual theory. The homunculus is called the mind, and because it is conceived as a conscious entity within the person, it is postulated that it must be aware of the source of any information it uses. There is widespread acceptance today of information being effective in perception without the perceiver being able to report its source, but there is still a tendency to treat "cues" that are below the level of consciousness as special cases requiring special terminology and special principles for their explanation. The interest in "subliminal" perception (Key, 1973) is an example of this tendency.

The Cue Concept

The view that depth cannot be perceived directly has persisted into modern psychology. The perception of three-dimensional space with eyes having light-sensitive surfaces that are two-dimensional has been regarded as a paradox. Osgood (1953) discussed this problem under the heading "The Paradox of Three-dimensional Perception." The paradox was stated in the form of a question: "Since the distribution of radiant energies on the retina is two-dimensional, how can we perceive depth and distance? [p. 248]" This is closely analogous to the question of how we can perceive an upright world with an inverted retinal image. Osgood restated the problem in a manner that assumed that a flat retinal image is the starting point for visual perception: "What additional cues or what dynamic properties of two-dimensional images give rise to three-dimensional experiences? [p. 249]" The experimental psychology of depth perception has, until quite recently, been the study of these cues. The cues have been treated as additional pieces of information which, when added to a flat picture on the back of each eye, make depth perception possible. It has been commonly assumed that in the absence of all such cues, only the two-dimensional qualities of optical stimulation would be experienced.

THE CLASSICAL CUES

During the period following the introduction of the eye–camera analogy, accommodation and convergence were regarded as the principal cues to depth. Both of these cues are associated with muscular activity in the visual system. The convergence of another person's eyes is directly observable, as shown in Figure 1.6. When a distant object is fixated, the lines of sight are nearly parallel and the pupils are at the centers of the eyes. When a near object is fixated, the lines of sight converge toward that object and the pupils appear nearer to the nasal sides of the eye. Early writers, such as Berkeley, believed that feedback from the muscles controlling the positions of the eyes was used to assess the distance of fixated objects. This is the "inflow" interpretation of convergence. More recent writers (Skavenski & Steinman, 1970) have presented evidence that it is not the feedback from these muscles that is used in depth perception, but rather it is information about the signals sent from the brain to the muscles in order to achieve and maintain varying fixations. This is the "outflow" interpretation. Convergence is currently regarded as a minor cue to depth, effective mainly for gross near–far discriminations at distances

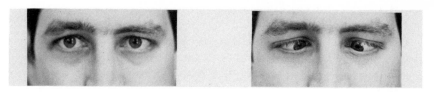

FIGURE 1.6. Convergence of the eyes during fixation on a distant object (left) and on a near object (right).

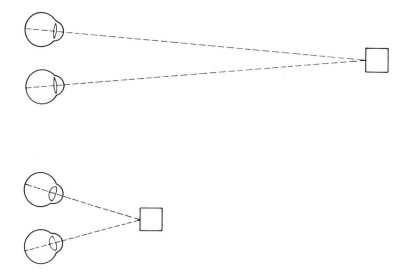

FIGURE 1.7. Convergence of the eyes during fixation on a distant object (top) and on a near object (bottom).

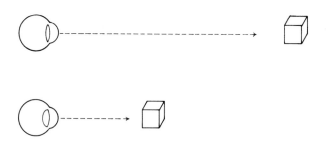

FIGURE 1.8. Accommodation of the lens during fixation on a distant object (top) and on a near object (bottom).

not exceeding several yards (Graham, 1965, p. 504). The geometry of convergence is illustrated in Figure 1.7.

Accommodation refers to the change in shape of the lens of the eye as objects at different distances are brought into focus (Figure 1.8). The focusing of images in the camera obscura by means of changes in the position of the lens was described by Porta. Even before the actual focusing mechanism in the human eye was discovered it was recognized that such a mechanism would have to exist and that it could indicate variations in distance. Like convergence, accommodation was originally regarded as an inflow mechanism, but has more recently been subjected to outflow interpretations. Also like convergence, accommodation appears to be effective only at relatively short distances.

The cue that has received the most attention in the psychological literature, binocular disparity, was described by Wheatstone in 1838. The images projected onto the retinas of the two eyes are different as a result of the separation of the eyes. This is illustrated in Figure 1.9. Wheatstone demonstrated that a realistic impression of depth can be obtained by presenting separate pictures to the two eyes, drawn from two viewpoints corresponding to the interocular separation. His prototype stereoscope is shown in Figure 1.10. The geometric basis of a stereogram is illustrated in Figure 1.11. A major addition to our knowledge of the role of binocular disparity in depth perception was produced recently by Julesz (1960, 1971), who showed that disparity was sufficient to indicate depth even in random dot patterns (Figure 1.12).

Convergence, accommodation, and binocular disparity have been traditionally referred to as the primary cues to depth. This is due to the belief that they provide direct sensory data that can be combined with the two-dimensional pictures on the retina, allowing these pictures to be interpreted as representing a scene in three-dimensional space. Depth is, according to cue theory, added to the pictures on the retina by these three cues. A single, momentary retinal image does not by itself contain the information used by any of these three cues. (This is not completely true for accommodation, for the observer might judge depth on the basis of blur

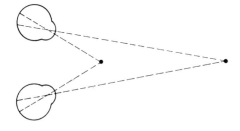

FIGURE 1.9. Disparity of the retinal projections of near and distant points.

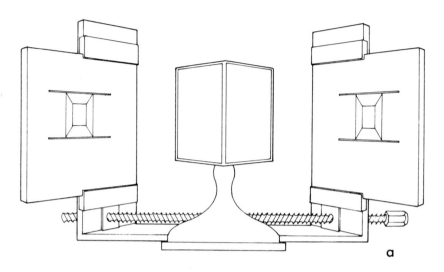

a

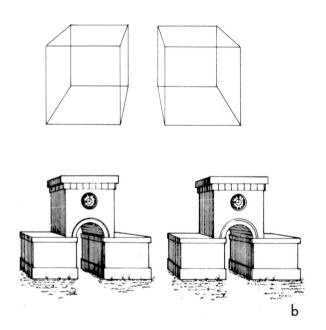

b

FIGURE 1.10.   (a) Wheatstone's stereoscope and (b) sample stereo pairs. The observer looks into the two mirrors at the center of the stereoscope. Each eye sees one of the two drawings mounted in the holders at either side.

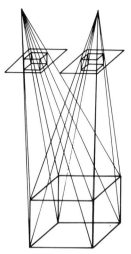

FIGURE 1.11. The projection of a three-dimensional object onto stereo pairs.

patterns for objects that are not accommodated. One may not wish to include such judgments in the definition of accommodation.) Similarly, these cues are not available in a photograph or in a painting. Differences in the images that a painting projects onto the two retinas are not affected by the distances represented in the painting. Viewing a painting involves approximately the same degree of convergence and accommodation throughout regardless of the distances represented. Yet it is well known that depth can, to some extent, be represented in a painting.

Depth perception in paintings and photographs has been explained by resorting to "secondary" or "pictorial" cues to depth. Figure 1.13 illustrates the cue of interposition. The top and bottom figures in each group appear to be in front of the middle figure. This is because the top and bottom

FIGURE 1.12. A random dot stereogram of the type introduced by Julesz.

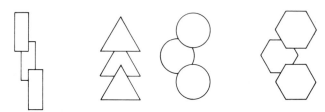

FIGURE 1.13.   Interposition.

figures appear to be complete while the middle figure appears to have its contours partially hidden by the other two figures. When one contour appears complete and appears to interrupt another contour, the complete contour is usually perceived as closer than the interrupted contour.

The relative distance of pictured objects may be judged by comparing their relative sizes in the picture to their relative sizes in three-dimensional space. This is the cue of relative size (Figure 1.14). Even when the objects are not of known size, the sizes of their representations in the picture may be used to judge relative distance. The objects in Figure 1.15 have identical representations except for size. They may be perceived as representing objects of the same size at different distances, although the alternative perception of objects differing in size and located at the same distance is also likely in the absence of other indicators of relative depth.

Linear perspective (Figure 1.16) refers to the convergence in a picture, or in a projection on the retina, of lines that are parallel in three-dimensional space. The role of perspective in depth perception will be considered in detail later, and linear perspective will be discussed as a special case of perspective in static scenes. Other cues that have been described include the height of an object above the line of sight in a picture (Figure 1.17), shadow (Figure 1.18), relative brightness (Figure 1.19) and atmospheric attenuation (Figure 1.20). All of these apply to the stationary observer viewing a stationary scene.

Until quite recently there has been only one cue considered by perceptual theorists that involves motion, either of the observer or of parts of the visual scene. This is motion parallax. When the eye moves from one position to another, as shown in Figure 1.21a, the rate at which the projection of an object moves across the retina varies with the distance of the object. A closer object will move faster, a distant object more slowly. Similarly, if two objects move in three-dimensional space at the same rates, the projection of the nearer object will move more rapidly across the retina (Figure 1.21b). This is the extent to which dynamic factors have been included in the traditional list of depth cues.

The concept of perceiving three-dimensional space through the use of

FIGURE 1.14. Relative size of familiar objects.

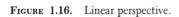

FIGURE 1.15. Relative size of similar objects.

FIGURE 1.16. Linear perspective.

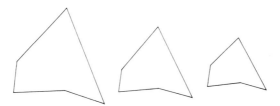

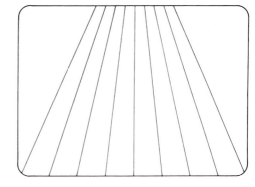

FIGURE 1.17. Relative height.

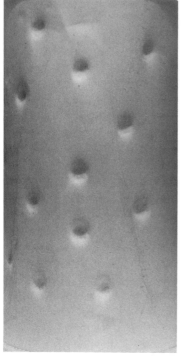

FIGURE 1.18. Shadow. Turning the book upside down inverts the apparent direction of illumination in the picture, causing the indentations to be perceived as protrusions.

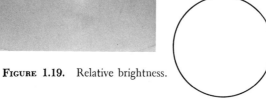

FIGURE 1.19. Relative brightness.

FIGURE 1.20. Atmospheric attenuation. The mountains appear closer in the clear view (top) than in the hazy view (bottom).

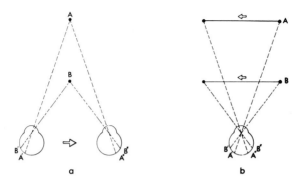

Figure 1.21. Motion parallax based on (a) left to right motion of the eye, and (b) right to left motion of the objects.

cues is a by-product of the eye–camera analogy. It is the homunculus in the brain who must combine these cues with the two-dimensional pictures he receives from the eyes to produce judgments about the relationships of objects in depth. The role given to the homunculus in this theory is like that of an air traffic controller. The controller observes a radar scope that provides a two-dimensional representation of the air space under surveillance. He must obtain information about the third dimension, altitude, from other sources such as radio transmissions from the aircraft. He combines the information from the radar display with the altitude information in order to make judgments about the paths that should be taken by the aircraft, which he then communicates to the pilots. The air traffic controller analogy is simply a modern version of the eye–camera analogy, complete with a two-dimensional picture, a homunculus and cues. It might be noted that there is an alternative air traffic control system that could be conceptualized in which information from sensors capable of detecting the positions of aircraft in three-dimensional space would be fed into a computer. The computer would contain a set of procedures designed to handle all of the contingencies expected in the air traffic environment. The procedures would be automatically applied to the input, taking into account other relevant inputs and information from its memory. The application of the procedures would produce a set of commands to be transmitted directly to the controls of each aircraft. This alternative system operates without the need of a picture or of a human controller.

Evidence against the Primacy of Flatness

The implied homunculus is not the only difficulty with the concept that three-dimensional perception results from the addition of cues to the retinal image. According to this concept, the perception of flatness is primary and the perception of depth is derived from an initial impression of a flat picture-like image. There are two implications of the primacy of two-dimensional perception that have been subjected to experimental investigation. The first implication is a developmental one. It is that a child or other young animal, before learning to associate the flat retinal image with the cues required for three-dimensional perception, will lack depth perception. Recent experimental evidence contradicts this postulate. The presence of depth perception with little or no prior experience was demonstrated by Gibson and Walk (1960) using an apparatus they call the "visual cliff." The visual cliff is essentially a table with a glass top divided lengthwise by a narrow board. On one side of this board, the "shallow" side, a sheet of patterned material is placed against the underside of the glass. On the other side of the board, the "deep" side, the same material is placed some distance below the glass (Figure 1.22). If an animal placed on the center board was responding only to the tactual qualities of the glass surface, it would have no reason to prefer moving to one side or the other. An animal responding to the relative distances of the patterned surfaces, which could only be discriminated visually, would be expected to prefer the shallow side. Gibson and Walk tested chicks, goats, kittens, rats, turtles, and human infants on the cliff as soon as they were capable of independent locomotion. All of these species preferred the shallow

FIGURE 1.22.   The visual cliff.

side. Two possible indicators of the relative visual depth of the two sides were described by Gibson and Walk. One is the relative density of the textures projected onto the retina of the subject. When the same objective texture was used on both sides, a coarser texture was projected by the visually shallower side. The second indicator is motion parallax. As the animal moved its head, the texture elements on the shallower side moved across the retina more rapidly than did those on the deep side. When the projected texture variable was controlled by using a coarser texture at the greater distance from the glass, animals tested without prior visual experience (rats reared in darkness and day-old chicks) still showed significant preference for the shallow side. This suggests that there is an innate ability in at least some animals to use relative motion as an indicator of differential depth.

CUES TO FLATNESS

The second implication of the postulated primacy of two-dimensional perception can be studied with adult human observers. This implication is that a visual scene should take on an increasingly flat appearance as depth cues are systematically eliminated. When all depth cues are eliminated, the scene should appear two-dimensional. This seems, at first, to be true at least for the type of stimulus materials and viewing conditions usually used in psychological research. An individual member of a stereo pair will appear flat when viewed directly, outside of the stereoscope. This is true for the meaningful material studied by Wheatstone (1838), shown in Figure 1.10, as well as for the random dot stereograms studied by Julesz (1971), shown in Figure 1.12. Shadow projections of texture elements moving across the screen at different velocities (to be discussed in later chapters) appear two-dimensional when motion is eliminated. Cue theory would hold that apparent flatness was due to the elimination of binocular disparity in the first case, and to the elimination of motion parallax in the second case. There is strong evidence against this interpretation. The mere elimination of cues to depth does not result in the perception of flatness. The tendency to perceive a scene as being represented on a flat surface is associated with specific sources of information in the scene. Woodworth and Schlosberg (1954) refer to these as "cues to flatness" and note that the experience of depth in a picture is enhanced by removal of "the restraining influence of negative cues [p. 469]." The presence of a visible frame around the scene is one such cue. Its effect can be dramatically demonstrated with a good quality color television picture. The viewer looking at the television screen monocularly through a tube that obscures its borders may experience an impression of depth as realistic as that obtained in direct vision. There is another indicator of flatness remaining in the television picture: the texture of the surface on which the picture is displayed. A uniform surface texture is an important indicator of flatness, especially in drawings and photographs. There are other negative cues that can be described as negations of the positive depth cues previously enumerated. A flat surface viewed binocularly may appear flat as a result of the uniform disparity of points in the projections of the surface onto the two retinas. There would also be a uniformity in the convergence angle of the two eyes as the surface was scanned. If the screen were sufficiently close, the information that there was no change in the shape of the lens during scanning of the display might contribute to an impression of flatness.

In studies in which the elimination of depth cues leads to judgments of flatness, some or all of these cues to flatness are present. Consider the example of a single member of the stereo pair in Figure 1.10. Observed directly, we find it framed by the borders of the page, printed on a textured sheet of paper and, if observed binocularly, presenting uniform disparity and convergence to the two eyes. If the same member of the stereo pair were displayed to both eyes in a stereoscope, the borders of the page would be concealed and the effect of background texture would be minimized. The reduction in the effect of texture uniformity would be reduced because the textures of the portions of the paper on which each member of the pair is printed would not match. Under these viewing conditions, an impression of depth can be produced with only one member of a stereo pair and, consequently, without binocular disparity. Smith and Gruber's (1958) research with photographs of three-dimensional scenes has shown that "compelling and highly realistic impressions of objects in depth" can be induced with monocular viewing and restriction of the field of view to the photograph (p. 307). Stereoscopic viewing of identical random dot patterns is less likely to create an impression of depth than is stereoscopic viewing of the type of drawing in Figure 1.10, because each pattern consists of a uniform, even texture.

The perception of flatness in the shadow projections to be described in later chapters is based on the same types of information as is flatness perception in drawings and photographs. If the screen on which the shadows are displayed is viewed binocularly, uniform disparity and uniform convergence will indicate that it is a two-dimensional surface. Even if monocular observation is used, the border around the screen and possibly the texture of the screen will indicate flatness. The procedures for creating a maximum impression of depth in a picture projected onto a screen are well known. They are designed to eliminate all indications of the flatness of the screen:

1. Viewing should be monocular to eliminate stereoscopic information which indicates flatness (uniform disparity) and any effects of uniform convergence.
2. The screen should be viewed from a distance of six feet or more to minimize the effectiveness of accommodation as an indicator of uniform distance of the screen.[3]
3. The screen should have a texture too fine to be detected at the six-foot viewing distance.

These procedures can be used to create realistic impressions of depth, especially with motion pictures.

Another way to test the proposition that the flat retinal projection is perceived in the absence of depth cues is to eliminate all known cues to depth and all known cues to flatness. This can be accomplished by totally eliminating patterned vision, producing an area of uniform visual stimulation surrounding the subject's eyes. This area, called a Ganzfeld, may be produced by having the subject fixate the center of a wall painted a homogeneous flat white, with all seams, corners, and edges concealed. Alternatively, it may be produced by covering each eye with a hemisphere that diffuses the surrounding illumination and has no visible texture of its own. Halves of ping pong balls approximate these specifications (Figure 1.23). With the illumination dim enough to prevent detection of inhomogeneities in the Ganzfeld, subjects report seeing a diffuse, space-filling fog

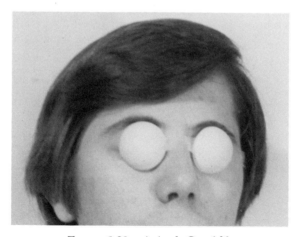

FIGURE 1.23. A simple Ganzfeld.

[3] A collimator lens is sometimes used to optically simulate an infinite viewing distance.

(Avant, 1965). This is a clear example of three-dimensional perception in the absence of patterned vision. It directly contradicts the theory that depth perception requires the addition of cues to an initially flat image.

RETINAL GRADIENTS

The concept of depth cues has not only failed to include cues to flatness but has not adequately handled the sources of information that are probably most important in the everyday perception of three-dimensional space. These are the gradients emphasized by James J. Gibson (1946):

The Retinal Gradient of Texture. Most surfaces contain visible textures. There are the man-made textures in the carpeting or linoleum on the floor; in a grass lawn, the texture elements are the individual blades of grass. In the projection of a surface onto the retina, both the projected sizes of the texture elements, such as the blades of grass, and the projected spacing between the elements vary with the distance of the elements from the eye (Figure 1.24). Cue theory holds that the relative size of the texture elements in the retinal projection serves as a cue to relative distance; Gibson, on the other hand, argues for a higher order relationship in which the retinal gradient serves directly as an indicator of a receding surface.

The Retinal Gradient of Size-of-Similar-Objects. This is similar in effect to the texture gradient, except that it refers to objects, usually familiar objects, that do not form a texture. Spacing between objects is not relevant in this case. This gradient is illustrated in Figure 1.25.

The Retinal Gradient of Velocity during Movement of the Observer. As the eyes move, points in the visible scene are displaced across the retina. The closer the points are to the eye, the more rapid the displacement. This is an important generalization of the motion parallax cue. Motion parallax had been studied with a small number of moving points, often only two. Gibson pointed out that in normal vision there is a continuous gradient of velocity which is directly related to the perception of surfaces in depth. This gradient is produced even by the slight eye movements that occur in normal vision and is therefore continuously available as an indicator of depth.

The Retinal Gradients Arising from Atmospheric Transmission of Light. This refers to the gradual decrease in the sharpness of the retinal projection with increased distance due to atmospheric haze (and more

FIGURE 1.24.   A naturally occurring texture gradient.

recently, to smog). It had been previously described as a depth cue, usually called aerial perspective, but had not been formulated as a gradient. This gradient was illustrated in Figure 1.20.

The Retinal Gradient of Binocular Disparity. Some stereograms, like those in Figure 1.12, display only two distances; normal vision encompasses continuous variations in distance which are represented by gradients of disparity in the retinal image. Figure 1.26 illustrates a disparity gradient in stereo photographs and Figure 1.27 illustrates such a gradient in a random dot stereogram.

The study of these gradients, particularly of texture and velocity gradients, has played an important role in recent research on depth perception. We will return to these gradients in later chapters.

FIGURE 1.25. A gradient based on sizes of similar objects.

Conclusion

The popular analogy between the eye and the camera has heavily influenced modern thinking about visual perception. The idea that perception begins with a flat, stationary image is implicit in much of the research and theory in this area. It is manifest in such questions as "How do we per-

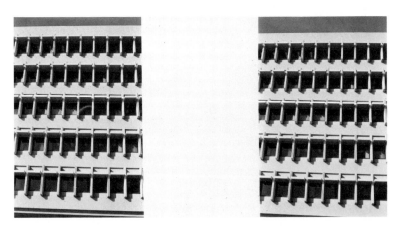

FIGURE 1.26. A disparity gradient based on a continuous increase in the distance between the building and the camera (from the bottom to the top of the photographs).

FIGURE 1.27. A disparity gradient in a random dot stereogram, based on aniseikonic distortion (see Chapter 5).

ceive the shape of an object to be relatively constant when its retinal shape varies with the object's slant?" and "How are successive views of a moving object combined to create the impression of a continuous transformation?" The view that the perception of motion in depth is at least as primary a perceptual experience as the perception of static flatness is a relatively new one. Partially for this reason, and partially because of the greater technical difficulty of research in that area, research on motion in depth perception is also relatively new.

Much of the research on depth perception currently reported is presented in terms of cues to depth. The cue concept has serious inadequacies. It does not normally include indicators of flatness or retinal gradients. It does not adequately handle the role of transformations in depth perception. We could broaden the cue concept to encompass these additional sources of information, but the connotation of a cue being used by a homunculus in the brain to interpret a flat retinal image is deeply ingrained in perceptual theory. It will be best to avoid the term "cue" in discussing current research.

Totally avoiding the homunculus problem will be more difficult. The homunculus idea is reflected in the tendency to regard the discovery of the sources of information required for accurate perception as the total problem of the perceptual researcher. It is as if a homunculus, once given the necessary information, can be counted on to make the appropriate judgments. The problem of considering the manner in which the information is processed has not been given adequate attention. Perceptual processes exist that operate on incoming information, usually leading to accurate perceptions of the external world. These processes may be inappropriate to certain stimulus conditions, leading to what have been called illusions.

If perceptual theory is to free itself from the homunculus concept it must be possible, at least in principle, to fully specify these processes. This will be our objective here, although it is one that cannot be fully realized with our present state of knowledge. We shall return to a consideration of the nature of perceptual processes in the final chapter, after we have examined the body of research on the perception of depth through motion.

2

Early Observations: Illusions of Motion in Depth

PRIOR TO THE SYSTEMATIC STUDY of motion as an indicator of depth, information about the role of motion in depth perception came primarily from reports of various illusions. The earliest of these reports were of situations in which motion in three-dimensional space was directly observed but the direction of motion was sometimes incorrectly perceived. The windmill, fan, and rotating trapezoid illusions are examples of illusions of misperceived direction of rotary motion. There were other cases, reported somewhat later, in which motion in depth was perceived in the absence of physical motion in depth. Lissajous and stereokinetic patterns are examples of objectively two-dimensional stimuli that may elicit perceived depth. In these cases, it was the appearance of motion in depth itself that was regarded as illusory. These two classes of illusions form the basis for much of the later systematic research on the perception of depth through motion.

The Windmill and Fan Illusions

There is a case of misperceived rotary motion in depth in which the incorrect perception is so compelling that it has created practical problems. In 1860 Sinsteden (Boring, 1942) reported an observation of a windmill silhouetted against the bright evening sky. The direction of rotation of the arms appeared to reverse repeatedly as he observed the windmill, and he could not tell whether he was looking at the front or the back of the mill. The similarity of the silhouettes for the front and back views is shown in Figure 2.1. Assume that the arm with the highest and leftmost silhouette in these figures is moving in a direction that will cause its silhouette to merge with that of the mill house. If the silhouette of the mill were taken as a front view (a) and (b), the arms would have to be rotating counterclockwise on the windmill's shaft. If the silhouette were that of a rear view (c) and (d), the merging of the arm silhouette with the house silhouette would have to be the result of a clockwise rotation. Sinsteden reported that he could cause himself to perceive one direction of rotation or the other by imagining himself on one side or the other of the windmill. The practical problem caused by the "windmill illusion" was noted by Miles (1929): There were instances in which purchasers of windmills believed that their mills were actually reversing in direction and complained to their windmill salesman that the equipment was defective.

Kenyon (1898) reported a similar effect from a two-bladed electric fan. He describes "a curious illusion" in which the apparent direction of rotation of a fan is sometimes opposite from the real one, and reports the illusion occurred at a viewing distance of 30 feet and at a "moderate" rotation speed. The effect, Kenyon notes, does not occur at closer distances or slower speeds. The apparent direction of rotation could be made to change at will, according to Kenyon's report. This is similar to what Sinsteden reported for the windmill, although Kenyon did not seem to be aware of the earlier report. Kenyon reported two additional observations that he made during the rotation of the fan: First, that the two blades of the fan appeared to flap together rather than rotate, and, second, that the two blades appeared to be continually withdrawing into and pushing out from the hanging rod. The observed fan was not actually a silhouette, but there was probably little information available at that viewing distance and rotation speed beyond that available in a silhouette.

Miles (1931) used a shadow projection apparatus to study the perception of the silhouette of a rotating fan. A two-bladed fan was placed between a projection lamp and a milk glass window (Figure 2.2). The subject viewed the shadow of the rotating fan from the opposite side of

FIGURE 2.1. The basis of the windmill illusion. Direct light and silhouette views are shown of the front (a) and (b) and rear (c) and (d) of the windmill. Note the similarity of views (b) and (d).

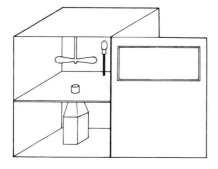

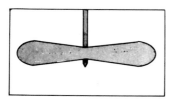

FIGURE 2.2. An early shadow projection apparatus (top) and the silhouette observed by the subject (bottom).

the window. Miles called this a "model for demonstrating the windmill illusion," recognizing the relationship between the windmill and fan illusions. In the first of two experiments, Miles asked naive subjects to describe the stimulus materials, recording any changes that occurred. All of his 27 subjects reported seeing rotary motion at some time and all but two subjects reported both the correct and illusory directions of rotation. Most of the subjects also reported the stretching and clapping effects noted by Kenyon. In a second experiment, which immediately followed the first one, Miles suggested various movement interpretations to the same subjects as they observed the shadow of the rotating fan. He asked the subjects whether they could see clearly the suggested motion within 15 sec after the suggestion. No more than two subjects responded "No" to this question for the four motions that had been most often described in the first experiment: correct rotation, reverse rotation, stretching, and clapping.

The Rotating Trapezoid

The best known case of misperceived rotary motion in depth is probably the rotating trapezoid illusion. Ames (1951) designed a trapezoidal window (Figure 2.3a) that resembled a rectangular window viewed from an

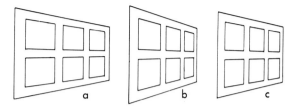

FIGURE 2.3. A trapezoidal window shown (a) in a front view, (b) with the left side slanted 45° towards the observer, and (c) with the left side slanted 45° away from the observer.

angle. When viewed monocularly from a sufficient distance, the rotating trapezoidal window appeared to be oscillating. Unlike the unpredictable reversals found in the windmill and fan illusions, the apparent reversals of direction were predictable for the trapezoid. The direction of rotation was correctly reported during the 180° of rotation for which the longer side was closer to the observer (Figure 2.3b), and incorrectly reported during the 180° for which the shorter side was closer (Figure 2.3c). When a rectangular window was rotated under the same viewing conditions, the direction of rotation was correctly reported throughout the 360° cycle.

Lissajous Figures

In each of the illusions described so far an object was actually rotating in three-dimensional space. The observer looked directly at the object or at its shadow. People who work with oscilloscopes are usually familiar with a case of apparent motion in depth in which there is no real object in motion. When two oscillators are connected to an oscilloscope, one to the horizontal and one to the vertical input, and are adjusted to frequencies in simple numerical ratio, Lissajous patterns result. These are looped patterns which appear on the face of the scope. They vary in complexity as a function of the ratio of the frequencies used. A 1:1 ratio produces a circle; a 2:1 ratio produces a two-looped figure, etc. (Figure 2.4). By slightly mistuning the frequencies, the patterns can be set into apparent motion. They may be perceived as rotating about a vertical or horizontal axis, depending on which input receives the higher frequency.

Rotating Lissajous patterns were introduced into the psychological literature by Weber (1930). He did not use the oscilloscope method because of its technical difficulty at that time. Instead, he used two electrically driven adjustable tuning forks. A small mirror was attached to the end of one prong of each fork. One fork was vibrated horizontally, the other vertically. A focused beam of light was set up that would

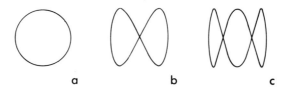

FIGURE 2.4.   Lissajous patterns produced by sine waves in (a) 1:1, (b) 2:1, and (c) 3:1 ratios.

strike one mirror, then would be reflected onto the other mirror and finally onto a silver screen. The Lissajous patterns could be varied by adjusting the frequencies of the tuning forks, which of course had the same function as the oscillators in the oscilloscope method. Weber reported subjective impressions of a 1:1 Lissajous pattern rotating about a vertical axis. He noted that the pattern may appear to rotate in depth with the apparent direction reversing from time to time. He also reported "it is easy to compel the figure to rotate" in a desired direction. This is similar to the reports of involuntary and voluntary reversal of direction with the windmill and fan illusions. Weber related his observations to reversable perspective in static figures, although he did not make the connection between Lissajous patterns and other cases of reversal of motion in depth.

Philip and Fisichelli (1945) studied Lissajous patterns as an instance of reversible figures, noting their relationship to the windmill illusion as well as to such static figures as the Necker cube and staircase (Figure 2.5). Working some 15 years later than Weber, they found the oscilloscope method to be more readily handled than the tuning fork method. They studied the effects of rotation speed and number of loops in the pattern on the rate of apparent reversal for patterns that appeared to rotate about a vertical axis. Increased pattern complexity and, to a lesser

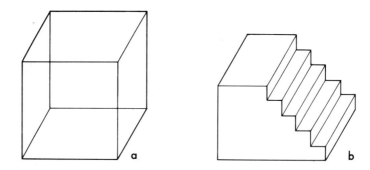

FIGURE 2.5.   Reversible static figures: (a) the Necker cube, and (b) the staircase.

degree, increased speed were found to increase reversal rate. In addition to rotary motion, their subjects reported a "wiggle" type of movement, sometimes described as an "accordion-like" movement. Fisichelli (1946) used the same method to study the effect of axis of rotation and height–width ratio of the pattern. He found more reversals with apparent rotation about a vertical axis than about a horizontal axis. Increasing the dimension of the pattern perpendicular to the axis of rotation decreased the reversal rate. Reports of "wiggle" again occurred.

The Stereokinetic Effect

A variety of two-dimensional patterns appear three-dimensional when rotated about an axis parallel to the line of sight (Figure 2.6). This

FIGURE 2.6.   Viewing arrangement for the stereokinetic effect.

instance of the perception of depth through motion is called the "stereo-kinetic" effect (Musatti, 1924, 1931). Metzger (1953, Ch. 13) gives a number of interesting examples of this effect (Figure 2.7), in which the patterns are made up of ellipses. Each of these examples has reversable perspective to at least some degree. Which part of the figure appears closer to the observer seems to depend on which part is fixated as the figure rotates. Duchamp (Schwarz, 1969) and more recently Duncan (1975) have produced works of kinetic art based on the stereokinetic effect. Three examples of Duncan's work, each of which produces dramatic depth effects when rotated, are shown in Figure 2.8.

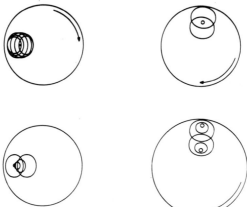

FIGURE 2.7. Elliptical patterns producing the stereokinetic effect. [After Metzger, 1953.]

FIGURE 2.8. Kinetic art of Fred Duncan, based on the stereokinetic effect.

Conclusion

One general finding that can be gleaned from these early and scattered reports of illusions is that the perception of motion in depth can take place without a clear perception of which parts of the moving object are approaching and which are receding. The perception of depth in rotating objects and the perception of direction of rotation appear to involve different perceptual processes affected by different sets of stimulus variables. The systematic study of these two issues will be handled separately in Chapters 4 and 6.

3

The Optic Array

THE INFORMATION WE USE IN visual perception reaches the eye, in almost all cases, as reflected light. There are a few exceptions in which a light source such as the sun, a flame, or the filament of a lamp is viewed directly, but in all other cases light is reflected by the surfaces that surround us. There is a pattern of reflected light converging on every point in three-dimensional space. Figure 3.1 shows one such pattern for one particular point. The point is located toward the left of the figure. Only the boundaries of surfaces are shown. Rays representing reflected light are drawn between the selected point and each surface boundary. Gibson (1966) calls this pattern of rays an optic array. The optic array contains information that is potentially available for visual perception. The optic array of interest in visual perception is one in which the rays converge at the eye. Figure 3.2 illustrates this array. It is similar to that shown in Figure 3.1, except that an observer is now included in the illustration. The observer's field of view is, as shown in Figure 3.2,

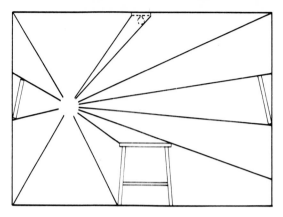

FIGURE 3.1. The main boundaries of the stationary optic array. [After Gibson, 1966.]

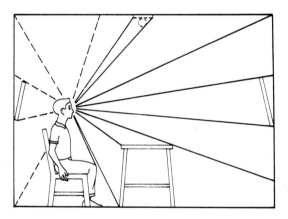

FIGURE 3.2. The effective array at a stationary convergence point. [After Gibson, 1966.]

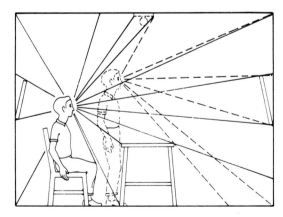

FIGURE 3.3. A transformation of the optic array obtained by a movement of the observer. [After Gibson, 1966.]

limited to a portion of the total optic array. The portion of the optic array that can enter the eye at any given time will be called, after Gibson (1966), the effective array.

Normally eyes are not stationary. Small, involuntary eye movements occur continuously. Larger eye movements associated with changes in fixation, as well as head and body movements, occur frequently. Whenever the eye moves, the effective optic array changes. In Figure 3.3, the observer's eye has moved to a new position, but the locations of the surrounding surfaces have not changed. It can be seen that the effective optic array has changed as a result of the change in position of the eye. It is with such transformations of the optic array, and with the role that they play in the perception of three-dimensional space, that we will be concerned in the remainder of this book. Information obtained from motions of the observer or of objects in the effective array, rather than information contained in static views, will be of primary interest. Although we have begun our discussion with surface boundaries, the role of surface texture elements in depth perception will be emphasized as we proceed.

This chapter will present a description of the information available for perceptual processing in the effective optic array and especially in transformations of the effective array. (For examples of mathematical analyses of this information, see Baird, 1970, and Hay, 1966.) It is important to keep in mind that a description of this information does not constitute an explanation of visual perception. Which of the sources of information potentially available in the optic array are actually used by the human observer and how information from these sources is processed are empirical questions. Describing the array is only a start in seeking answers to those questions. Research directed at obtaining these answers will be the subject of subsequent chapters.

The Projection Plane

The optic array has been defined in terms of a point at which rays of reflected light converge. For the effective array this is the focal point of the eye, as shown in Figure 3.2. Before the information in the optic array can be used in perceptual processing it must be projected onto the surface of the retina. Our description of the optic array will be concerned with this retinal projection. Rather than dealing directly with geometric relationships on the curved surface of the retina, we will use a convenient approximation described by Leonardo Da Vinci (Richter,

1952). Da Vinci proposed that it would be useful for the painter to think of a plane of glass located between his eye and the scene he is attempting to reproduce on canvas. The glass plane would be perpendicular to his line of sight, as shown in Figure 3.4. A tracing of the outlines of objects as they intersect this glass would reveal the approximate relative proportions of the retinal surface occupied by the projections of these objects. This plane has been called a picture plane by some and an image plane by others. We will use the designation projection plane, to emphasize that our description of this plane is for the purpose of presenting the geometry of optical stimulation. The projection plane is a geometrical abstraction, not a picture or an image to be apprehended by a homunculus in the eye or brain.

The dimensions of an object's representation on the projection plane is determined by a combination of factors: (1) its dimensions in three-dimensional space; (2) its orientation to the observer; and (3) its distance from the observer. Simple illustrations of these factors are provided in Figure 3.5. In drawing (a) we have two objects at the same distance from the observer. The object on the left is twice as large in its horizontal

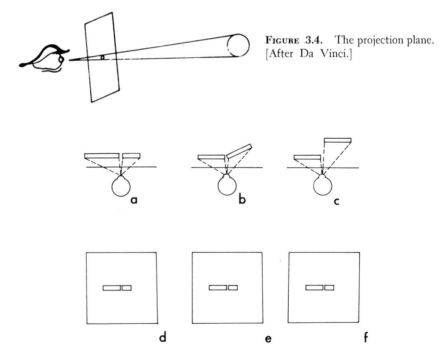

FIGURE 3.4. The projection plane. [After Da Vinci.]

FIGURE 3.5. The effects of (a) size, (b) orientation, and (c) distance on the projection plane representations (d,e,f) of objects.

dimension as the object on the right. It follows that the projected width of the object on the left will be twice that of the object on the right. This can be seen in the frontal view of the projection plane (d). In drawing (b), both objects are the same size and at the same distance, but the object on the right is at a slant with respect to the observer's line of sight. For the particular slant angle illustrated, the projected width of the object on the left is again twice that of the object on the right (e). Finally, in drawing (c), the two objects have the same horizontal dimension, but the one on the right is twice as far from the observer. The projected width of the object on the left is again twice that of the object on the right (f). The effect of the distance between the observer and an object on the dimensions of that object's projection is a perspective effect. In general, perspective refers to variations in a two-dimensional projection of a three-dimensional scene that reflect relationships in the third dimension.

Perspective Gradients

The perspective variation example given above involved a comparison of two measurements in the projection plane, the horizontal extents of the projections of two objects. In the projection of a more complete visual scene, perspective variations usually would not consist of such discrete changes but would instead be reflected in continuous, gradual changes. We will refer to these gradual changes as perspective gradients.

Texture Gradients

The retinal gradient of texture, described in Chapter 1, is a perspective gradient available in everyday perception. Visual scenes usually consist of surfaces that vary in their distance from the observer and that have visible textures (Figure 3.6). These textures are formed by surface features, ranging from wood grain and other irregularities in smaller surfaces viewed from short distances to blades of grass, rocks, brush, and trees in larger surfaces viewed from greater distances. Figure 3.7 shows examples of textured surfaces found in natural environments. In most naturally occurring surfaces, texture elements vary both in size and in separation. Both these variations in the size and spacing of surface features may be regarded as aspects of texture, although they can be considered separately and have been studied separately in the laboratory.

FIGURE 3.6. The textured surfaces in an everyday visual scene.

A texture gradient is formed when a textured surface is represented on the projection plane. Figure 3.8 shows a uniform random texture and a projection plane representation of a uniform texture at an angle of 60°. A plot of the 60° gradient, showing the average separation between the projections of texture elements as a function of the distance of the elements from the observer, is presented in Figure 3.9.

LINEAR PERSPECTIVE

What has been called the cue of linear perspective is a special case of a texture gradient. Linear perspective occurs when two parallel lines are present in some plane in the effective array, and this plane is slanted (i.e., neither perpendicular nor parallel) with respect to the line of sight. Figure 3.10 illustrates a typical source of linear perspective. The observer is looking at the ground plane, which contains two parallel lines. These lines appear on the projection plane as two converging lines. The systematic decrease in the distance between the two lines on the projection plane, going from the bottom to the top of that plane, constitutes a

Figure 3.7. Examples of naturally occurring textures.

47

FIGURE 3.8. A uniform random texture at angles of (a) 0° and (b) 60° to the frontal plane.

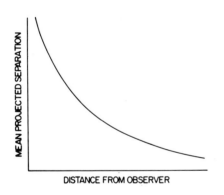

FIGURE 3.9. A 60° texture gradient. (The simulated viewing distance is 2.6 times the width of the projection plane.)

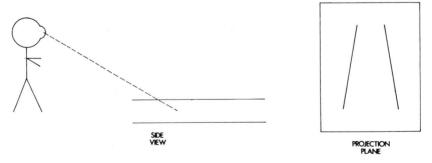

FIGURE 3.10. Linear perspective.

gradient. The gradient is presented graphically in Figure 3.11. The horizontal axis in this plot displays distances from the eye to positions on the ground plane. The vertical axis represents separations between the converging lines in the projection plane. Each point on the curve indicates the separation of the converging lines in the projection plane that corresponds to a given distance between the observer's eye and the ground plane. The reader should compare Figure 3.11 to Figure 3.9. The two functions are identical. Both the projections of parallel lines and the projections of randomly distributed surface features carry the same perspective information. This does not mean that both stimulus situations are identical for the observer. As indicated earlier, we are discussing the geometry and not the psychology of depth perception in this chapter. The manner in which observers utilize the information available in the optic array is an empirical question which will be considered in later chapters.

If the reader wishes to further satisfy himself that the same information is contained in Figures 3.8b and 3.10b, he can use the following procedure. (1) Place tracing paper over Figure 3.8b, and draw a vertical line down the center of the figure (Figure 3.12a). (2) Draw a horizontal line (Figure 3.12b) at the bottom of the vertical line, which is equal in width to the separation of the lines at the bottom of Figure 3.10b. (Draw the horizontal line where it will be bisected by the vertical line.) (3) Count the number of texture elements crossed by the horizontal line on each side of the vertical line in Figure 3.8b and take the average of these two numbers. (4) Count a number of elements equal to that average on each side of the vertical line at the top of Figure 3.8b (Figure 3.12b). Draw a horizontal line through these elements. Connecting the horizontal lines should produce approximately the same two converging lines as

FIGURE 3.11. Linear perspective as a gradient.

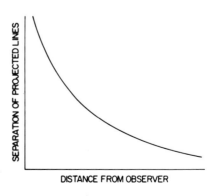

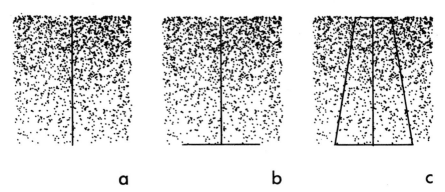

a   b   c

FIGURE 3.12. Procedure for showing the correspondence of a texture gradient and a linear perspective gradient. (The illustration is idealized. Had the horizontal lines actually been based on counting dots, the match to linear perspective would not have been as exact, due to the random variability in the dot pattern.)

in Figure 3.10b (Figure 3.12c). This relationship between linear perspective and texture gradients would be no surprise to the artist, because both gradients are based on the same principles of perspective. The patterns in Figure 3.8b and Figure 3.10b are, in fact, both fully determined by the location of a single point, the vanishing point. This is shown in Figure 3.13.

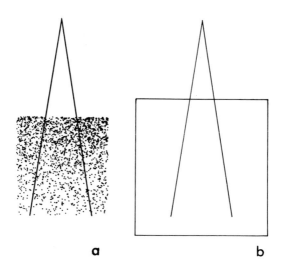

a   b

FIGURE 3.13. The vanishing points for corresponding texture and linear perspective gradients.

REGULAR TEXTURES

The texture elements in most naturally occurring surfaces vary randomly in size and spacing, but some man-made surfaces have texture elements that are equal in size, in spacing, or in both. Figure 3.14a shows such a regular texture in the frontal plane. Figure 3.14b is a projection plane representation of this texture in which the top of the surface is slanted away from the observer. This figure demonstrates an important characteristic of regular textures viewed at a slant: The projections of these textures contain the converging lines associated with the projections of parallel lines. Going from random to regular textures means going from the indirect availability of linear perspective as a source of depth information to its direct availability or, more precisely, to its increased availability. The availability of this information is increased because the number of lines converging to the same vanishing point is greater in the projection of a slanted surface of a regular texture, as compared to the two lines usually used to define linear perspective.

MOTION PERSPECTIVE

The perspective gradients we have considered so far are represented in the projection plane as spatial variations. These are variations in the sizes and spacing of the projections of objects or texture elements simultaneously present in the effective array that reflect their distances from the observer. There is another type of perpective gradient that will be of primary interest here. This is the gradient that occurs over time, when movement of the observer or of an object being observed alters the distance between the observer and the object. Gibson has aptly labeled this type of perspective gradient as motion perspective. Consider the example of an observer moving directly towards an object on which he is fixating.

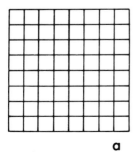 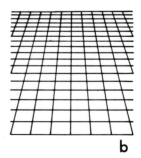

a   b

FIGURE 3.14. A regular texture (a) in the frontal plane, and (b) at a 60° slant.

The projection of the object on the retina will grow as the observer moves. Figure 3.15 illustrates this transformation. The top part of the figure shows the changes in the observer's position and the resulting changes in the optic array. The bottom part of the figure presents a series of projection plane representations of the object as the observer approaches it. Unfortunately, there is no way to show the reader a continuous transformation. We are limited to displays of successive stationary views. This limitation of our medium, a book, must not be taken to imply that it is useful to think of the perception of a continuous transformation as consisting of a series of static views.

Perspective variations occurring over time can, like spatial variations, be displayed as gradients. The transformation shown in Figure 3.15 is presented as a gradient in Figure 3.16. The horizontal axis indicates the distance between the observer and the object. The vertical axis indicates the width of the object's representation on the projection plane. (Other dimensions of the projection could have been used as well.) A point on the curve displays the projected width corresponding to the distance of

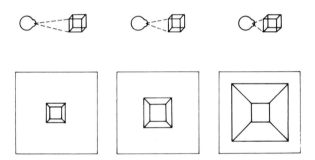

FIGURE 3.15. Changes in the projection of an outline cube with the approach of an observer.

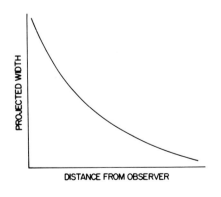

FIGURE 3.16. A motion perspective gradient based on Figure 3.15.

the object, at a given time during the transformation sequence. The crucial difference between this plot and the type of gradient plot presented earlier (Figure 3.9) is that the horizontal axis in this plot represents a temporal rather than a spatial variation in the distance between the observer and the object.

As a second example, consider an observer who is moving to his left and looking straight ahead during this motion. The principal changes in the projection of an object, as shown in Figure 3.17, would be in the relative positions of its contours rather than in the projected sizes of the contours. The closer contours move farther across the projection plane than do the more distant contours in a given period of time. This, of course, means that the closer contours move faster. This aspect of motion perspective has traditionally been called motion parallax. Figure 3.18 shows this transformation as a perspective gradient.

The changes in the representation of an object in the optic array that

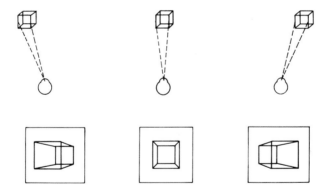

FIGURE 3.17. Changes in the projection of an outline cube obtained from a right to left motion of the observer.

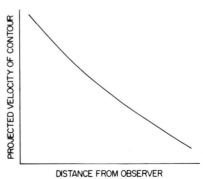

FIGURE 3.18. A motion perspective gradient based on Figure 3.17.

are produced by motions of the observer can also be produced by motions of an object in relationship to a stationary observer. In terms of the geometry (not the psychology) of vision, bringing an object closer to an observer has the same effect as bringing the observer closer to the object. The projections in the bottom part of Figure 3.17 could have been produced by the situation shown in Figure 3.19. Here the observer is stationary and the object is moving. The changes in the projection of the object that resulted from the observer's right to left head movement (Figure 3.17) could also have resulted from the object being moved from left to right (Figure 3.19).

In everyday vision, most transformations of the optic array result from motions of the observer's eyes because most of the surfaces that surround us belong to inanimate objects. Most laboratory studies of transformations of the optic array, on the other hand, use a stationary observer and a moving object. This is because it is easier to control the motion of an object, using a motor or an animated motion picture, than it is to control the motion of an observer's eye. It is also somewhat easier to describe the changes in the projections of objects as these objects undergo various motions, and to illustrate these motions diagrammatically, than it is to describe and illustrate observer motions. Transformations in the optic array will be described in this chapter in terms of object motions. As we consider research on the perception of these transformations in subsequent chapters, it should be recognized that the results of studies of object

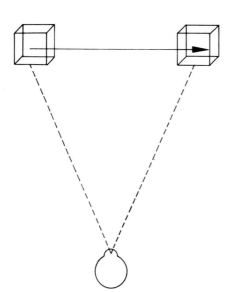

FIGURE 3.19. An object motion that would produce the same projections as the observer motion in Figure 3.17 and the same gradient as in Figure 3.18.

motions do not necessarily apply directly to situations in which the
observer is in motion.

Parallel Projections

Before we proceed with a detailed description of the changes in the
optic array that occur with motions of objects in the visual field, there
is a special type of two-dimensional projection of a three-dimensional
scene that should be considered. This projection would occur if the eye
were so far from an object being observed that the relative distance from
the eye to parts of the object had no effect on the projection of the
object. For this condition to hold precisely, the eye would have to be
infinitely far from the object. This is of course impossible, but the
situation can be approximated with sufficiently great distances. An object
far enough away to eliminate the effects of the relative distances of its
parts on its projection would be barely visible in direct vision, but
viewing conditions of this type occur when a telescope is used. The optic
array resulting from these viewing conditions is illustrated in Figure 3.20.
The most significant feature of this array is that the rays from the
contours of the distant object are parallel, giving rise to the designation
"parallel projection." In a parallel projection, the point at which a
ray intersects the projection plane is unrelated to the distance between
the eye and the contour from which the ray is drawn. This may be
contrasted to the type of projection previously illustrated, called a
polar projection. In a polar projection the point at which a ray from a
contour intersects the projection plane is determined, in part, by the distance between that contour and the eye.

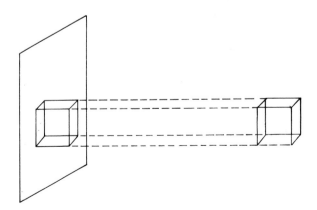

Figure 3.20. A parallel projection of an outline cube.

Because parallel projections are unaffected by variations in the third dimension, they can be said to lack perspective. The principles of perspective illustrated above do not apply to parallel projections. In parallel projections, objects identical in size in three-dimensional space have the same projected size regardless of their distance from the observer. There is no detectable expansion of the projection of an object as the observer approaches it, as long as the observer's distance from the object is sufficiently great so that it may be treated as infinite. (Only astronauts have experienced detectable increases in the size of the moon as a result of approaching it.) When the eye is moved laterally, all parts of the object move across the projection plane at the same rate (Figure 3.21).

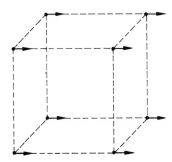

FIGURE 3.21. The motion of a parallel projection of an outline cube during a right to left observer movement.

These characteristics of parallel projections have made such projections of particular interest to researchers in visual perception. Parallel projections are used in the laboratory to isolate changes in the optic array that are not related to perspective variations. These projections can be approximated using a shadow technique with a distant light source, or precisely generated using computer animation. Because of their importance in perceptual research, parallel projections as well as polar projections will be included in the following discussion of the manner in which transformations in three-dimensional space are represented on the projection plane.

Rigid Motions in Three-Dimensional Space

Of the infinite variety of motions that can occur in three-dimensional space, a subset of six motions has received the most attention in perceptual research. These are the rigid motions of rotation and translation with respect to three orthogonal axes.[1] The axes are conveniently defined as follows: The Z (depth) axis is the observer's line of sight; the X (horizontal) axis is parallel to the line connecting the two eyes and per-pendicular to the line of sight; the Y (vertical) axis is perpendicular to both the X and Z axes. The three axes are illustrated in Figure 3.22. In general, the origin will be the observer's fixation point. The following sections will consider rotations about the Y and Z axes and translations along the X and Z axes. The geometry of rotation about the Y axis applies equally well to the X axis, with appropriate interchanging of the symbols X and Y and the words horizontal and vertical. Similar sub-stitutions can be made in the discussion of translation along the X axis. (The Y axis is sowewhat more common in rotation studies; the X axis is more common in translation studies.) Three stimulus examples will be used to describe the projections produced by each rigid motion: (1) two

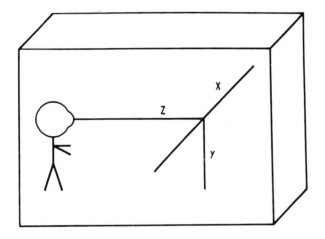

FIGURE 3.22. Labels to be used for the three orthogonal axes.

[1] These transformations will be classified in accordance with their occurrence in three-dimensional space rather than in accordance with changes in the retinal pro-jection. This is different from Gibson's (1954) classification, which described retinal changes. Gibson's first four retinal transformations — translation, rotation, size trans-formation, and perspective transformation — result from translations and rotations in three-dimensional space. Specifically, Gibson's translation is associated with the present X and Y translations, his rotation with the present Z rotation, his size transformation with the present Z translation, and his perspective transformation with the present X and Y rotations.

dots[2] initially at different distances[3] from the observer; (2) a two-dimensional texture; and (3) a three-dimensional texture.

ROTATION ABOUT THE Y AXIS: POLAR PROJECTION

The projection of each element in a pattern rotating about the Y axis traces an elliptical path on the projection plane. This can be readily seen in the two-dot example (Figure 3.23). For a more detailed examination of this path, it will be convenient to divide it into two parts: The projection of the element during the semi-cycle (180°) of rotation when it is farther from the observer will be labeled Part A; the projection during the semi-cycle when it is closer to the observer will be called Part B. The elliptical path projected by a rotating dot can be seen to have the following characteristics: (1) Part A of the projected path is closer to the X axis than is Part B. (2) Part A is less curved than is Part B. In comparing the elliptical paths of the two dots, the following additional characteristics can be noted: (3) The path of the top dot, which is closer to the X axis in three-dimensional space, is relatively narrower than the path of the bottom dot, which is more distant from that axis (i.e., the minor axis of that path is relatively shorter); and (4) the path of the bottom dot, which is closer to the Y axis in three-dimensional space, is shorter than the path of the top dot, which is more distant from that

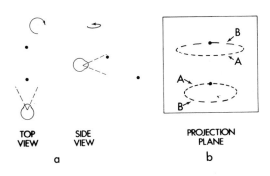

TOP   SIDE   PROJECTION
VIEW   VIEW   PLANE
        a   b

FIGURE 3.23. Rotation about the Y axis, parallel projection: two dots at different distances from the observer.

[2] The dots will be treated as markers for points in three-dimensional space and on the projection plane. Consequently they will not vary in size in the illustrations. Our interest is limited to variations in position and velocity. We will not be concerned with variations in the sizes of texture elements in this chapter.

[3] The distances from the observer referred to in these sections, unless the context clearly indicates otherwise, are measured from the eye to the XY plane of the texture element rather than directly to the element. They are, in other words, differences between the Z coordinate of the eye and the Z coordinate of the texture element.

axis (i.e., the major axis of that path is shorter). Each of these four characteristics of the elliptical paths is a perspective effect. Each reflects changes in the distance between the observer and the dot, as the dot rotates in depth.

In addition to these perspective effects on the projected paths, there are perspective effects on the projected velocities of the dots. These are reflected in the relative lengths of the dashed segments in Figure 3.23c. In general, the closer a dot is to the observer, the greater is the velocity of its projection. This is only generally true because there is another factor that also affects the velocity of a projected dot. A rotating dot, unlike the translating dots to be discussed below, does not maintain a constant linear (straight line) velocity in three-dimensional space. In the examples used here, and in virtually all studies of rotary motion, the pattern moves at a constant *angular* velocity throughout the transformation. The definition of angular velocity is illustrated in Figure 3.24a. The angle of interest is that formed by connecting two successive positions of the dot with the axis of rotation. Rotation at a constant angular velocity means

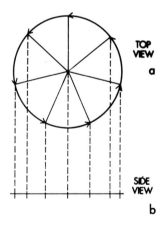

FIGURE 3.24. The conversion of a constant angular velocity to sinusoidal horizontal position changes.

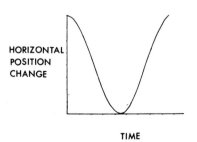

that this angle will be the same for any two positions of the dot, provided that these positions are recorded at equal time intervals. Put another way, the change in this angle is constant over time. When a dot is rotating about the Y axis with a constant angular velocity, its horizontal location is a cosine function of time. This is illustrated in Figure 3.24b. For each time interval, the change in the horizontal position of the dot is determined by the cosine of the angle through which it has rotated. A graph of this function is presented in Figure 3.24c.

The cosine factor applies only to the horizontal position of the projected dot. It operates independently of the effects of perspective. A change in the projected horizontal position of the dot is determined by the product of a perspective factor and a cosine factor. The vertical position, on the other hand, is affected only by a perspective factor. The perspective factor is the same for both the horizontal and vertical coordinates of the projected dot. This gives the following results:

$$
\begin{aligned}
\text{horizontal change} &= \text{perspective factor X cosine,} \\
\text{vertical change} &= \text{perspective factor, therefore} \\
\frac{\text{horizontal change}}{\text{vertical change}} &= \text{cosine,}
\end{aligned}
$$

where a *change* is defined as the ratio of the present horizontal or vertical coordinate of the projected dot to a previous coordinate. Figure 3.25 illustrates this relationship.

The cosine factor and the perspective factor are potentially separable in a two-dimensional projection of a rotating dot. This is an important point, because the two factors carry different information about the motion of the dot. The cosine factor implies that the dot is moving at a constant angular velocity, i.e., is rotating. It does not indicate direction of rotation. The cosine of an angle lacks directional information because the cosine of a positive angle is the same as that of a negative angle of

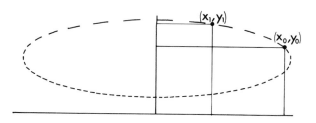

FIGURE 3.25. Derivation of the angle of rotation from the change in projected position of a dot. The initial position is (x_0, y_0). The new position is (x_1, y_1). The cosine of the angle of rotation about the Y axis is given by $(x_1/x_0)/(y_1/y_0)$.

the same magnitude. In contrast, the perspective factor does include directional information. The velocity of the dot and the distance of its projected path from the X axis are generally greater when the dot is closer to the observer. If the dot is moving from left to right, for example, and these perspective effects indicate that it is in the closer portion of its path, that path (in an overhead view) would have to be clockwise. At this point in our discussion, the cosine factor should be regarded only as a potential indicator of rotary motion in depth, and the perspective factor as a potential indicator of direction of rotation. Whether the human observer extracts and uses the information in these ways is an empirical question which will be addressed in later chapters.

As a second example of rotation about the Y axis, consider a textured plane undergoing this transformation (Figure 3.26). The left side of the texture is approaching the observer in the illustrated sequence (Figure 3.26b). The projection of this side expands during the transformation in both the horizontal and vertical dimensions. The projection of the right side contracts in both dimensions. These are perspective effects. At the same time there is an overall horizontal compression of the projected texture. This occurs as the plane deviates from a frontal position, regardless of the direction of rotation. The maximum compression occurs when the plane is rotated to an angle of 90° with respect to the frontal position. At this angle its projection is a vertical line, as shown in Figure 3.26b. This overall compression is unrelated to the distance between the observer and the rotating textured plane, and is therefore not a perspective effect. It is a reflection of the cosine factor, described previously. As in the two-dot example, the cosine factor affects only the horizontal positions of the projected texture elements while the perspective factor affects both the horizontal and the vertical positions. The ratio of the horizontal to the vertical change in the projected position of a texture element (these changes themselves expressed as ratios) yields the cosine of the angle through which the surface has rotated.

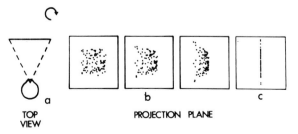

TOP VIEW   PROJECTION PLANE

FIGURE 3.26. Rotation about the Y axis, polar projection: a textured plane with the left side approaching the observer.

As a three-dimensional example, consider a texture made up of dots within the confines of an unseen sphere (Figure 3.27). The spherical pattern is of particular interest in perceptual research because it does not display edges during rotation, as does the textured plane. The projections of individual texture elements move in the same way as do those in the previous example, however there is no two-dimensional expansion or contraction of portions of the texture observable in static projections. There is also no overall horizontal compression of the projected texture. This is because every location on the projection of a sphere represents the same range of locations in depth as the sphere rotates. There is no way to distinguish among static views of a rotating sphere on the basis of texture density. The only indication of rotary motion in successive static views would be the change in position of recognizable clusters of texture elements, if such clusters are present (Figure 3.27). In a dynamic view of a rotating sphere, the velocity variations based on the cosine factor are available as potential indicators of rotation in depth while velocity variations based on the perspective factor, described in the two-dot example, are available as potential indicators of the direction of rotation.

ROTATION ABOUT THE Y AXIS: PARALLEL PROJECTION

In a parallel projection of an object rotating about the Y axis, changes in the positions of texture elements are determined solely by the cosine factor. The change in the horizontal position of the projection of a texture element, expressed as a ratio, is determined by the cosine of the angle through which that element has rotated. There is no change in the vertical position of a projected element during rotation. Figure 3.28 illustrates a parallel projection of two rotating dots. The path of each dot on the projection plane is a horizontal line. The position and velocity

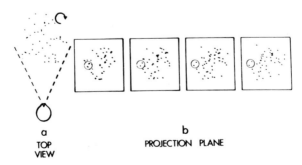

a
TOP
VIEW

b
PROJECTION PLANE

FIGURE 3.27. Rotation about the Y axis, polar projection: a three-dimensional texture. (The same two dots are circled in each projection plane view.)

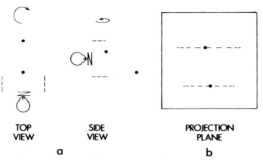

FIGURE 3.28. Rotation about the Y axis, parallel projection: two dots at different distances from the observer.

of the projected dots are not affected by their distances from the observer. There is no information in the path or in the velocity that could indicate whether the dot was traveling in the half-cycle closer to the observer or in the more distant half-cycle. There is, consequently, no information in the projection from which direction of rotation could be determined. This is true for the two- and three-dimensional texture examples as well. The only changes in the projection of a rotating textured plane (Figure 3.29) or in a rotating spherical texture (Figure 3.30) are in the horizontal positions of the projected texture elements.

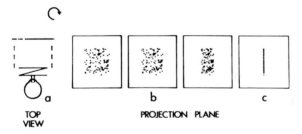

FIGURE 3.29. Rotation about the Y axis, parallel projection: a textured plane with the left side approaching the observer.

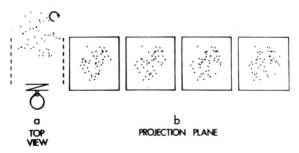

FIGURE 3.30. Rotation about the Y axis, parallel projection: a three-dimensional texture.

ROTATION ABOUT THE Z AXIS: POLAR PROJECTION

In this transformation the projection of each pattern element travels in a circular path at a constant angular velocity. This is illustrated in Figure 3.31 for the two-dot example. The closer dot projects a larger path, which means that it moves across the projection plane at a greater velocity (as each dot traverses its path in the same time interval). These variations in the projected paths and velocities of the dots, resulting from differences in viewing distance, are perspective effects. There is also a nonperspective factor that can produce similar variations: If one dot is farther from the axis of rotation than the other, in the three-dimensional scene it will project a larger path even if both dots are the same distance from the observer. The closer the actual dot is to the axis of rotation, the closer its projection will be to the point at which that axis intersects the projection plane. This is illustrated in Figure 3.32. There is no way to distinguish between the effects of the perspective and nonperspective factors on the basis of a projection of a pattern rotating about the Z axis. (Notice that Figures 3.31b and 3.32b show identical paths.) If the projection of one dot

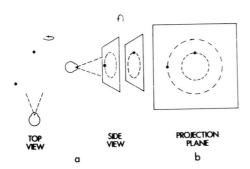

TOP VIEW   SIDE VIEW   PROJECTION PLANE

a   b

FIGURE 3.31. Rotation about the Z axis, polar projection: two dots at different distances from the observer.

FIGURE 3.32. Rotation about the Z axis, polar projection: two dots at the same distance from the observer but at different distances from the axis of rotation.

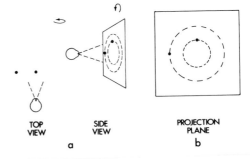

TOP VIEW   SIDE VIEW   PROJECTION PLANE

a   b

is closer to the axis of rotation than the projection of another dot, it may be because the first dot is closer to the axis of rotation in three-dimensional space, or because it is more distant from the observer, or because of some combination of these conditions. This is a general ambiguity associated with this transformation, regardless of the pattern displayed. As a result of this ambiguity, the projections of two-dimensional and three-dimensional textures rotating about the Z axis cannot be distinguished on the basis of the paths or velocities of the texture elements.

Figure 3.33 shows successive projection plane views of a two-dimensional texture rotating about the Z axis. A particular cluster of dots is circled in each view to show the direction of rotation. If the actual transformation were viewed, the observer might follow the motion of these or other projected dots. A three-dimensional texture rotating about the Z axis is shown in Figure 3.34. Note that there is no way to distinguish between the two- and three-dimensional textures on the basis of this transformation.

ROTATION ABOUT THE Z AXIS: PARALLEL PROJECTION

The two dots in the first example (Figure 3.31) share the same path in a parallel projection (Figure 3.35), which does not reflect the difference

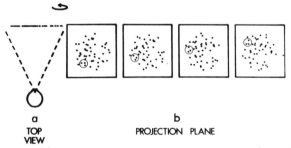

FIGURE 3.33.   Rotation about the Z axis, polar projection: a two-dimensional texture. (The same three dots are circled in each projection plane view.)

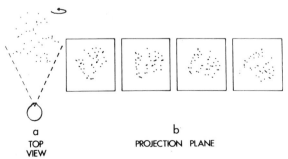

FIGURE 3.34.   Rotation about the Z axis, polar projection: a three-dimensional texture.

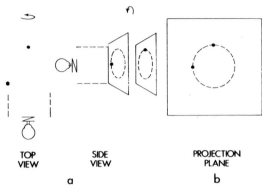

FIGURE 3.35. Rotation about the Z axis, parallel projection: two dots at different distances from the observer.

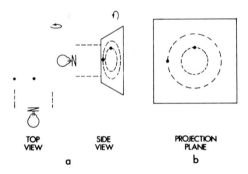

FIGURE 3.36. Rotation about the Z axis, parallel projection: two dots at the same distance from the observer but at different distances from the axis of rotation.

in their distance from the observer. The nonperspective factor illustrated in Figure 3.32, however, produces the same path differences in a parallel projection (Figure 3.36) as it did in the polar projection. Note that there are now three cases that are indistinguishable on the basis of the projected paths and velocities of two texture elements: the polar projection of dots at different distances from the observer (Figure 3.31); the polar projection of dots at different distances from the axis of rotation (Figure 3.32); and the parallel projection of dots at different distances from the axis of rotation (Figure 3.36). In addition, parallel projections of two- and three-dimensional textures (Figures 3.37 and 3.38) are indistinguishable from each other and from polar projections of either texture (Figures 3.33 and 3.34) undergoing this transformation.

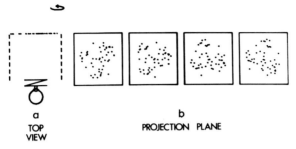

FIGURE 3.37. Rotation about the Z axis, parallel projection: a two-dimensional texture.

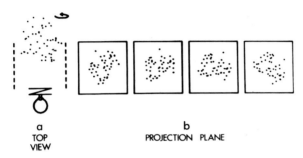

FIGURE 3.38. Rotation about the Z axis, parallel projection: a three-dimensional texture.

TRANSLATION ALONG THE X AXIS: POLAR PROJECTION

The projection of each element in a pattern undergoing this transformation moves horizontally across the projection plane. The path of each projected element is a straight line parallel to the X axis. Each projected element moves at a constant velocity throughout the transformation, but the projections of different elements may move at different velocities. The closer the pattern element is to the observer, the faster its projection will move across the projection plane.

In the first example (Figure 3.39a) two dots are moving from right to left relative to the observer. Figure 3.39b shows the projected paths of the dots during this translation. The projection of a dot moves a constant distance across the projection plane in each time interval. The dot that is closer to the observer covers a greater distance on the projection plane, indicating that its projection is moving more rapidly.

All the dots in the second example (Figure 3.40a) are the same distance from the observer. When the texture moves from right to left, all the projections of the dots travel at the same velocity across the projection plane. This is shown in Figure 3.40b.

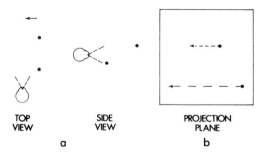

FIGURE 3.39. Translation along the X axis, polar projection: two dots at different distances from the observer.

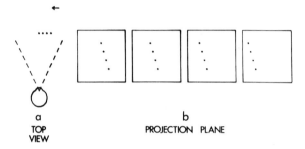

FIGURE 3.40. Translation along the X axis, polar projection: a two-dimensional texture.

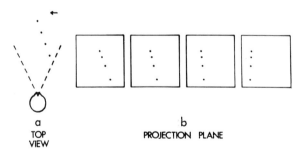

FIGURE 3.41. Translation along the X axis, polar projection: a three-dimensional texture.

In the third example (Figure 3.41a) the dots are at varying distances from the observer. The texture again moves from right to left. As in the first example, the projection of each dot moves at a constant rate, but these rates vary for the different dots in accordance with the distances of the dots from the observer. Projections of a three-dimensional texture translating along the X axis are shown in Figure 3.41b.

TRANSLATION ALONG THE X AXIS: PARALLEL PROJECTION

When a parallel projection of this transformation is displayed (Figure 3.42a) the projection of each pattern element moves at the same velocity. There is no effect from variations in the distances between the pattern elements and the observer on the projected velocities because all distances between the observer and the pattern are treated as infinite in a parallel projection. Figure 3.42b shows successive projections of two dots at different distances from the observer. Both the dots move exactly the same distance in each time interval, indicating that they are moving at the same velocity. This should be compared to the polar projection shown in Figure 3.39b, where the closer dot moved more rapidly.

The type of projection makes no difference in the two-dimensional texture example (Figure 3.43a). As in Figure 3.40b, all of the dots move at the same velocity across the projection plane (Figure 3.43b). In the polar projection, the dots were at a constant finite distance from the observer; in the parallel projection they are all at an infinite distance.

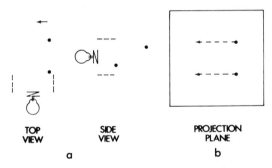

TOP VIEW   SIDE VIEW   PROJECTION PLANE

a   b

FIGURE 3.42. Translation along the X axis, parallel projection: two dots at different distances from the observer.

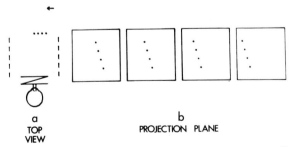

a
TOP VIEW

b
PROJECTION PLANE

FIGURE 3.43. Translation along the X axis, parallel projection: a two-dimensional texture.

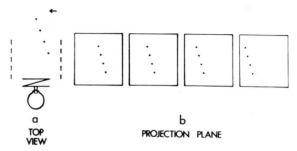

FIGURE 3.44. Translation along the X axis, parallel projection: a three-dimensional texture.

The projections of all of the texture elements in a three-dimensional texture (Figure 3.44) also move at identical velocities in a parallel projection. There is no way to distinguish, on the basis of the velocities of the texture elements, between a parallel projection of a three-dimensional texture, a parallel projection of a two-dimensional texture, and a polar projection of a two-dimensional texture.

TRANSLATION ALONG THE Z AXIS: POLAR PROJECTION

When a pattern is moving toward the observer, the projection of each element in the pattern moves away from one specific point on the projection plane. This is the point at which the line of sight intersects the projection plane. The path of each projected element is a straight line connecting the projection of that element to the projection of the origin (Figure 3.45). The velocity of a projected element is not constant; the projection of an element accelerates throughout the translation. The velocity at any given instant depends on two factors: (1) the distance of the element from the origin, in three-dimensional space, and (2) the distance of the element from the observer, in three-dimensional space. The acceleration of a projected element, however, depends only on the second factor. This is important because it means that there is information in the projected display that relates to the distance of pattern elements from the observer: The closer an element is to the observer in three-dimensional space, the faster its projection accelerates on the projection plane.

Figure 3.46a illustrates the two-dot example for translation along the Z axis. The dots are moving in paths parallel to the Z axis, toward the observer. The projections of the dots at equal time intervals are shown in Figure 3.46b. While both dots are traveling at the same velocities in three-dimensional space, their projections travel a greater distance in each suc-

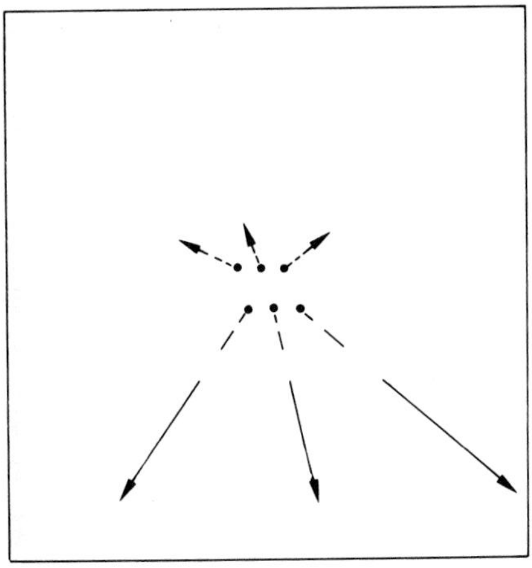

FIGURE 3.45. Paths of elements in the projection of a pattern moving toward the observer.

TOP VIEW   SIDE VIEW   PROJECTION PLANE

a   b

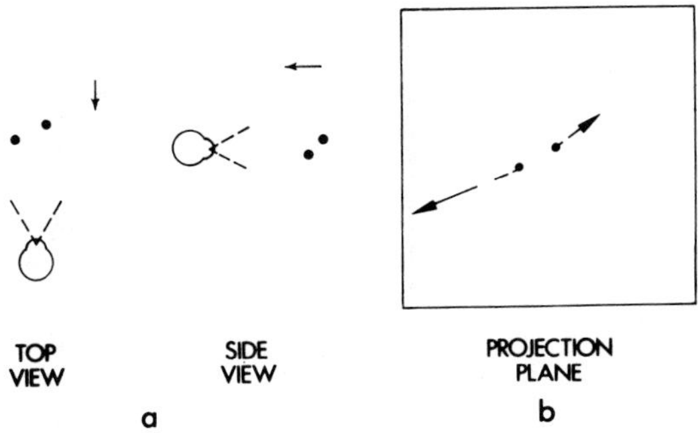

FIGURE 3.46. Translation along the Z axis, polar projection: two dots at different distances from the observer.

cessive view because both projections are accelerating. The change in the distance traveled between successive pairs of projection plane views is greater for the dot closer to the observer, indicating that the projection of this dot is accelerating more rapidly.

In the second example (Figure 3.47a), a textured flat surface perpendicular to the line of sight is moving toward the observer. The projection plane views (Figure 3.47b) show the expansion of the projected texture. The projected velocities of the elements vary, but the acceleration of each texture element is the same. When a three-dimensional texture moves toward the observer (Figure 3.48), the projected accelerations vary with the distances of the elements from the observer. The closer elements accelerate more rapidly. The difference between a uniform and a nonuniform acceleration of the texture elements is a potential basis for distin-

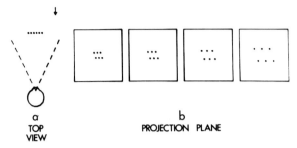

FIGURE 3.47.   Translation along the Z axis, polar projection: a two-dimensional texture.

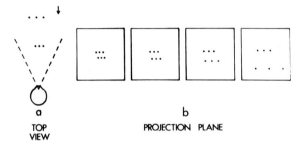

FIGURE 3.48.   Translation along the Z axis, polar projection: a three-dimensional texture.

guishing between polar projections of two-dimensional and three-dimensional textures that are approaching, or receding from, the observer.

TRANSLATION ALONG THE Z AXIS: PARALLEL PROJECTION

The projections of the pattern elements do not vary in position during this transformation when a parallel projection is displayed. This is true regardless of the nature of the pattern being transformed. The lack of motion in this projection is reasonable when we consider the meaning of a parallel projection of a pattern translating along the Z axis: The pattern is approaching, or receding from, the observer but it is always infinitely distant. Successive projection plane views of a parallel projection of any pattern undergoing this transformation would be identical.

Conclusion

This chapter has been concerned with the information potentially available in the paths and velocities of texture elements undergoing rigid transformations. Table 3.1 summarizes that information, as it relates to possible

TABLE 3.1
INFORMATION AVAILABLE IN RIGID TRANSFORMATIONS

			Direction	Dimensionality
Rotations	X	Polar	yes	yes
		Parallel	no	yes
	Y	Polar	yes	yes
		Parallel	no	yes
	Z	Polar	yes	no
		Parallel	yes	no
Translations	X	Polar	yes	yes
		Parallel	yes	no
	Y	Polar	yes	yes
		Parallel	yes	no
	Z	Polar	yes	yes
		Parallel	no	no

judgments of direction of motion and dimensionality of the texture. With this descriptive background on the information potentially available in the retinal projections of rigid transformations, we can proceed to a consideration of how the human observer uses this information. There are three major empirical questions that the next three chapters will consider in turn: (1) Under what circumstances do projections of transformations in three-dimensional space, and other dynamic retinal projections, elicit reports of motion in depth? (2) How does motion affect the accuracy with which the orientation of a surface to an observer can be judged? and (3) What information do observers use in judging the direction· of rotary motion, and how is this information processed?

4

Transformations Leading to the Perception of Depth

T HE PRECEDING CHAPTER CONSIDERED THE geometric relationships between rigid motions in three-dimensional space and projection plane representation of these motions. This chapter will examine the relationships that have been empirically determined between these projection plane representations and reported perceptions of motion in depth. There are two research strategies that have been used to select two-dimensional projections for study (Johansson, 1964). In one strategy, the researcher first determines which three-dimensional transformations are to be investigated and then produces two-dimensional projections representing patterns undergoing these transformations. Systematic variations are introduced in the type of pattern displayed (e.g., its regularity and dimensionality), in the viewing distance simulated in the projection, and in other factors believed to affect the perception of depth relationships in the projection. The objective is to determine which information available in the two-dimensional projections produced in direct vision is actually used by the human observer in the perception of three-dimensional space. Miles' (1931) study of the rotating fan illusion was a forerunner of this strategy, which has since been used by a number of investigators (Wallach & O'Connell, 1953; Gibson & Gibson, 1957; Green, 1961; Braunstein, 1962, 1966).

The second strategy is to produce systematic variations in the two-dimensional projections displayed to the experimental subject, without trying to represent specific three-dimensional transformations. This strategy provides a direct means of studying the way in which human observers use information available in two-dimensional projections. The forerunner of this strategy is the work of Weber (1930) and Philip and Fisichelli (1945) on Lissajous patterns. It has since been used mainly by Johansson and his associates (Johansson, 1950, 1964; Johansson & Jansson, 1968; Börjesson & von Hofsten, 1972, 1973).

If these two research strategies were employed in their purest forms they would each have serious drawbacks. Finding the processes by which the human observer goes from the information in two-dimensional projections of the optic array to perceived depth would be difficult if we were restricted to projections of real three-dimensional transformations. Only a limited range of stimulus variations occurs in accurate projection plane representations of direct vision. The search for systematic relationships between projection plane variations and depth perception often requires the study of ranges and combinations of variations that do not occur in direct vision. Failure to study these additional variations would severely limit research on the role of transformations of the optic array in depth perception.

The drawback of the second strategy is the complement of the drawback of the first. Studying variations in two-dimensional projections, without regard to whether these projections are related to those produced by transformations in three-dimensional space, could be unproductive. The investigator could become indefinitely involved with variations in the projection plane that have no relevance to normal depth perception. In practice, neither strategy has been applied in its pure form. Both have been modified to overcome these drawbacks. When actual transformations in three-dimensional space form the basis for the projections to be studied, modifications of these transformations are introduced that systematically alter the two-dimensional projections (e.g., Braunstein & Payne, 1968a). When variations in the two-dimensional projections are of primary interest, the variations selected for study usually are related to those found in direct perception of three-dimensional space (e.g., Johansson, 1974). The two research strategies, then, mainly reflect a difference in emphasis, and the results of studies using both strategies will be combined in the following section.

In general, the research in this chapter will be organized according to the transformations in three-dimensional space that are displayed or simulated. For studies in which specific transformations are not simulated, the dominant perception reported by subjects will be used to determine the sections in which the study will be discussed.

Rotations about the X or Y Axis

THE KINETIC DEPTH EFFECT

The perception of rigid motion in three-dimensional space by observers presented with shadows of rotating objects was demonstrated by Miles (see Chapter 2), although his work was not designed to explore the range of stimulus conditions that would elicit such perceptions. Such an exploration was carried out some years later by Wallach and O'Connell (1953). Their study was based on a concern for formulating rules of spontaneous perceptual organization from which predictions could be made as to which patterns of retinal stimulation will lead to the perception of flat figures and which will lead to the perception of three-dimensional forms. Wallach and O'Connell used a shadow projection technique similar to that used by Miles. A series of objects was placed between a point light source and a translucent screen and rotated about a vertical axis. The distance between the light source and the object was "made large [p. 206]," so that the projection on the screen approximated a parallel projection. The shadows of some of these objects appeared three-dimensional only when the objects were rotated. Static views of the shadows of these objects did not appear three-dimensional. It was therefore possible to isolate the effects of motion on perceived depth. Wallach and O'Connell assigned the term "kinetic depth effect" to this case of the perception of depth through motion. Eight of the experiments (1–5 and 7–9) in their classic study of this effect will be summarized below:

Experiment 1: Rotation of Solids. A solid block in the shape of a roof with sloping gables was displayed in continuous rotation about a vertical axis (Figure 4.1). Subjects described the stationary views as two-dimensional figures, but the dynamic view of the shadow of the rotating block elicited reports of a solid object rotating in depth. Perceived direction of rotation appeared to be a chance matter. Spontaneous reversals of direction occurred, including repeated reversals at 180° intervals. This ambiguity of perceived direction of rotation is typical of parallel or near parallel projections. The systematic reversal at 180° intervals is also found with certain plane figures, especially trapezoids. This experiment demonstrated

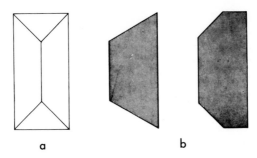

a   b

Figure 4.1. The solid block: (a) diagram, and (b) examples of the shadows. [After Wallach & O'Connell, 1953.]

that the perception of a solid object rotating in depth can occur even when the direction of rotation cannot be determined. This empirical finding should be compared to the geometric observation in Chapter 3 concerning the separability of depth and direction information. Subjects apparently can respond separately to these two kinds of information.

Experiment 2: Partial Rotation of Wire Figures. Two wire figures were studied. One was a "parallelogram" containing one diagonal. The wire figure was bent along this diagonal, so that the planes of the two halves formed an angle of 110° (Figure 4.2a). The second figure was a wire, bent twice, with one section in each of three planes (Figure 4.2b). The figures were turned back and forth through a 42° angle. Like the solid block, these figures appeared two-dimensional when stationary and three-dimensional when rotating. Most of the subjects correctly reported the shape of the first figure, but only a fourth of the subjects correctly reported the shape of the second figure. These results suggest that the perception of rotation in depth is, at least in part, independent of the correct perception of the shape of the rotating object.

FRONT VIEW   TOP VIEW

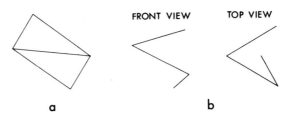

a   b

Figure 4.2. (a) The parallelogram, and (b) the wire "helix." [After Wallach & O'Connell, 1953.]

Experiment 3: Rotation of a Truncated Cylinder. Systematic cuts were made in wooden cylinders to produce shadows that expanded and contracted when the cylinders were rotated. Contour lines in such shadows change in length during rotation of the object, but do not change in orientation in the projection plane, as do the contour lines in the shadows of the solid object in Experiment 1 (compare Figure 4.3 to Figure 4.1). Subjects reported these shadows to look flat. On the basis of Experiments 1–3, Wallach and O'Connell reached the following generalizations: Shadows that expand and contract in only one dimension will be seen as dark figures changing in width. Shadows that display contours that simultaneously change in length and direction (orientation) will appear to be turning solid forms. These results seemed to imply that a simultaneous change in the length and angular orientation of a contour in a two-dimensional shadow is necessary and sufficient for depth perception in the transforming shadow.

Experiment 4: Rotation of Straight Rods. The sufficiency of a simultaneous change in the length and direction of a contour for eliciting depth perception was confirmed for shadows of a straight rod. The rod was fastened to a vertical shaft at an angle, to produce the desired changes in the shadow during rotation (Figure 4.4a). The reported perceptions were of motions in three-dimensional space, but the angle of tilt and path of motion were not correctly described by most subjects.

Experiment 5: Rotation of T and Triangle Figures. Further evidence that change in contour length alone is usually insufficient for depth perception came from the study of a rotating T figure (Figure 4.4b). Three-quarters

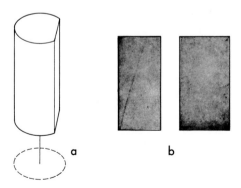

Figure 4.3. A truncated cylinder: (a) diagram, and (b) examples of the shadows.

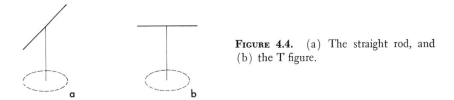

FIGURE 4.4.   (a) The straight rod, and (b) the T figure.

of the subjects reported seeing the horizontal bar expanding and contracting in the plane of the screen, and one-quarter of the subjects reported rotation in depth. The shadow of a rotating triangle, which does have contours that simultaneously change in length and direction, was described as rotating in depth by 17 of 20 subjects. Wallach and O'Connell suggested that the rotating T figure did not elicit depth perception directly even for the one-quarter of the subjects who reported rotation in depth. They held that depth perception based on a change in length alone must be due to past association of this type of stimulation with contours simultaneous changing in length and direction. As evidence, they reported that 15 of the 17 subjects who reported the triangle to be rotating in depth, when subsequently presented with the T figure, reported that figure to be rotating as well. This conclusion is certainly debatable. An alternative hypothesis is that simultaneous length and direction changes were more effective than changes in length alone in overcoming flatness indications present in the experimental situation, and past experience with these changes *in that situation* had a general facilitating effect on depth perception. It is likely that the same type of prior experience would increase the frequency of depth reports even when the simultaneous length and direction changes were present. In the case of the triangle, for example, 18, 19, or 20 of the subjects, instead of 17, might have reported rotation in depth if they had previously observed a shadow display that gave that appearance in the same experimental situation.

Experiment 7: The Effect of Angle Constancy.   The shadow of three rods all meeting at angles of 110° (Figure 4.5a) turning back and forth through an angle of 42° was shown to 56 subjects who had previously reported the stationary shadow of this figure to be two-dimensional. The shadow contained contours that simultaneously changed in length and direction. Fifty-three subjects reported seeing a three-dimensional object rotating in depth. When the shadow screen was covered with a circular aperture that concealed the ends of the rods at all times (Figure 4.5b), 22 naive subjects all reported seeing a flat figure which distorted. The aperture eliminated visible length changes in the contours, leaving only changes in direction. The lack of perceived depth with the aperture present was taken as sup-

FIGURE 4.5. Three rods meeting at 110° angles (a) with the ends of the rods visible, and (b) with the ends of the rods concealed. [After Wallach & O'Connell, 1953.]

port for the hypothesis that both changes must occur at the same time for depth to be perceived.

Experiments 8 and 9: Variation of Distances between Objects. Four spheres mounted on thin vertical rods were arranged at corners of a square concentric with the turntable. In Experiment 8 the rods were different heights, so that imaginary lines connecting the shadows of the spheres would simultaneously change in length and direction as the turntable revolved (Figure 4.6a). In Experiment 9 they were all the same height so that the lines would change in length only (Figure 4.6b). All of the 30 subjects in Experiment 8 reported the perception of motion in depth. Of 15 naive subjects in Experiment 9, only three reported three-dimensional perceptions. The hypothesis about contour changes was thus confirmed for imaginary lines connecting features of the transforming pattern. These lines, too, had to simultaneously change in length and direction to elicit reports of motion in depth from a majority of the subjects.

Evidence that depth perception in shadow patterns lacking simultaneous length and direction changes is based on past experience was presented in the report of a subsequent study of the kinetic depth effect (Wallach, O'Connell, & Neisser, 1953). Wire figures were displayed which were reported to appear two-dimensional when stationary by a majority of the subjects. When these figures were turned back and forth, most subjects reported perceptions of motion in depth. The subjects were again presented with the stationary shadows after an interval of from several minutes to a week. Most of the subjects now reported perceiving the stationary shadows as three-dimensional. Reversals of the Necker–cube type occurred after prolonged exposure to these shadows of stationary figures, indicating that the memory effect was not due merely to a ten-

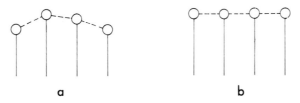

FIGURE 4.6. Imaginary lines connecting spheres displayed (a) at varying heights, and (b) at the same height.

dency to make three-dimensional reports when presented stationary views of figures previously shown in rotation.

The results of these two studies led to a clearly stated explanation of the perception of rotation in depth on the basis of projection plane representations of transforming figures: If the projection contains contour lines, real or imaginary, that simultaneously change in length and direction, a three-dimensional perception results. Depth perception in projection plane representations of stationary figures, or in projections having contours that change in length only or in direction only, was attributed to past experience with simultaneous changes. This explanation appears to be generally correct but perhaps too strongly stated. An alternative statement would be that the kinetic depth effect is strongest with simultaneous changes in length and direction but is also present when either change occurs in isolation. In the Wallach and O'Connell experiments, the kinetic depth effect was placed in conflict with indicators of flatness, such as the border of the screen, lack of binocular disparity, and lack of differential accommodation in viewing the screen. Elimination or reduction of these indications of flatness should have increased the number of depth reports for stimuli that displayed changes in length only or in direction only. Support for this hypothesis is found in some of the more recent studies of kinetic depth perception.

In one of a series of experiments concerned mainly with the accuracy of kinetic depth perception, White and Mueser (1960) found a considerably higher proportion of depth responses to shadows changing in length only than did Wallach and O'Connell. The display consisted of two pegs inserted into a turntable that rotated about a vertical axis. The pegs were located on a diameter of the turntable and were equidistant from its center (Figure 4.7a). The turntable was placed between a translucent screen and a distant light source, yielding an approximately parallel projection. The pegs were either identical in shape (Figure 4.7b) or different in shape (Figure 4.7c). The shape of the screen allowed the subjects to see the

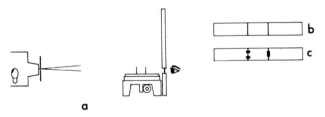

FIGURE 4.7. Method used to study the accuracy of kinetic depth perception: (a) apparatus, (b) identically shaped pegs, and (c) differently shaped pegs. [After White & Mueser, 1960.]

centers of the pegs at all times during rotation but not the tops of the pegs or the turntable. The displays were viewed under six conditions, combining three levels of fixation point (central, to one side of the display, above the display) and two levels of display orientation (horizontal or vertical). The mean duration of three-dimensional reports for each display exceeded half the observation period. This duration was greatest for fixation points to one side of the display, next greatest for fixation points above the display, and least for central fixation. Orientation of the display did not, by itself, affect the duration of these reports, although it did interact significantly with the fixation condition. The duration of three-dimensional reports was generally greater when the pegs were different in shape. The greater duration of depth reports for the distinguishable pegs (Figure 4.7c) compared to the identical pegs (Figure 4.7b) seems to support the Wallach and O'Connell explanation of kinetic depth perception. The shadows of the identical pegs contained no lines, real or imaginary, that changed in both length and direction. The shadows of the distinguishable pegs, on the other hand, did contain features that could be connected by imaginary lines which changed simultaneously in length and direction (Figure 4.8). There is, however, an interesting question of interpretation. Do the spheres set at different heights (Wallach and O'Connell's Experiment 8) and the distinguishable pegs generate more depth reports because of identifiability of elements or because of the simultaneous length and direction changes? Identifiability would itself tend to work against two-dimensional organizations of such stimuli. In the case of the two pegs, the most common two-dimensional report was of the pegs moving alternately toward and away from each other across the screen (see Figure 4.9). According to this report, when one of the pegs moved from the left (or right) to the center of the screen, the same peg would appear to move back to the left (or right) after its shadow merged with that of the other peg. The actual situation was that the shadows of the pegs crossed when they met, and the shadow that had moved from one side to the center continued to move to the opposite side. The crossing of the shadows is characteristic of projections of rigid configurations rotating in depth. The perception of the pegs as not crossing would therefore tend to support a two-dimensional organization of the display, while the perception of the pegs as crossing

FIGURE 4.8. Imaginary lines, connecting features of distinguishable pegs, that change in length and direction.

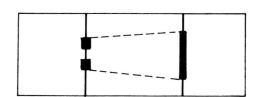

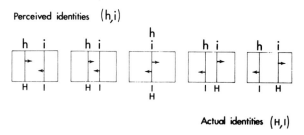

FIGURE 4.9. The most common two-dimensional organization reported for two pegs. The arrows show the direction of motion of the shadows. The upper case letters indicate the actual identities of the two pegs; the lower case letters indicate the perceived identities. A 180° rotation is diagrammed.

would support a three-dimensional organization. Information about whether the pegs crossed was lacking in the shadow projections of identical pegs. The displays of distinguishable pegs, on the other hand, provided a clear indication of the crossing of the pegs. It is likely that identifiability of display elements contributes to the perception of rotation in depth. Some indication of the effects of identifiability may be found in a comparison of the results of two of Wallach and O'Connell's experiments. In Experiment 5, the sides of the rotating triangle were not distinguishable but length and direction changes did occur. Three of 20 subjects reported two-dimensional perceptions in that experiment. None of the 30 subjects reported two-dimensional perceptions in their Experiment 8, in which the displayed spheres could be distinguished on the basis of differences in height. The number of two-dimensional reports with identifiability lacking is too small to form the basis for a firm conclusion, although these results are in keeping with the suggestion that there are at least two processes underlying increased reports of depth perception with identifiable display elements: (1) Simultaneous length and direction changes imply motion in depth, and (2) identifiability of display elements inhibits certain two-dimensional responses.

White and Mueser's findings of depth responses for more than half of the observation periods with shadows of identical pegs contradicts Wallach and O'Connell's hypothesis about the necessity of simultaneous length and direction changes for kinetic depth perception. Imaginary lines between the shadows of these pegs would change in length only. There are two likely reasons for White and Mueser's finding of depth perception with identical peg displays: (1) Their viewing conditions reduced indications of flatness. Subjects observed the screen monocularly through a prism, eliminating flatness perception due to lack of disparity and probably reducing the effectiveness of accommodation. (2) The subjects viewed all of the displays in the experiment in a counterbalanced order. Many of the responses to identical peg displays were made after the observation of distinguishable peg displays, allowing a memory effect to operate. According to Wallach and O'Connell (1953), depth perception in displays of shadows with contours that change in length only is enhanced by prior observation of displays with contours that change in both length and direction (see also Wallach, O'Connell, & Neisser, 1953).

COMPUTER SIMULATIONS OF ROTATIONS IN DEPTH

The shadow technique used in the studies discussed so far was valuable in the formulation of general hypotheses about perceptions of motion in depth, but it presented some disadvantages for more detailed studies of the basis of such perceptions. It is not possible, for example, to separate changes in the positions of contours of wire figures, pegs, and other objects from changes in the thickness of these contours. A distant light source minimizes but does not eliminate thickness changes. When a closer light source is used for producing polar projections, the thickness changes are obvious. Other problems with the shadow method include variations in the sharpness of the contours, especially when the object is close to the light source, and the necessity of using connected pattern elements which are physically anchored to a rotating device. (Objects cannot consist of lines or dots floating in space, for example, even if such patterns are desirable for studies of kinetic depth perception.) The drawbacks of the shadow technique can be overcome by using animated motion pictures. These motion pictures do not require the physical rotation of real objects and the display possibilities are therefore not limited by the need to attach each element to a mechanical device. As the experimenter determines exactly what will appear on each frame of the motion picture, unwanted variations in the thickness of contours and the sharpness of edges need not occur.

Computer animation was introduced into perceptual research by Green (1961). This method is more practical than hand animation because the individual frames of the motion picture are drawn automatically. More important, they are drawn directly from mathematical specifications, allowing the experimenter to exercise precise control over the stimulus materials. A computer program is written in which a three-dimensional pattern is represented by an array of X, Y, Z coordinates. The pattern is transformed by a mathematical operation on these coordinates. A rigid rotation, for example, can be produced by a matrix multiplication. The transformation is computed in discrete intervals, and a two-dimensional projection is computed at each interval. Each projection is displayed on a plotting device controlled by the computer (either directly or by means of instructions written on a magnetic tape). The plotting device, usually a cathode ray tube (CRT), is photographed and each photograph becomes a frame of a motion picture. In some cases the display is observed directly by subjects on the CRT, rather than photographed. (See Appendix A for further details on the computer animation method.)

Green (1961) conducted "a series of experiments designed to isolate the effect of relative movement from all other cues to depth and coherence [p. 272]." Patterns of dots, unconnected lines, or connected lines (Figure 4.10) were displayed undergoing one of two types of rotation: rotation about a fixed axis ("spinning"), which is the transformation used in all of the studies cited above, and rotation about a continuously changing axis ("tumbling"). Subjects were asked to rate the apparent rigidity or coherence of each display on a five-point scale, with coherence defined as the degree to which the elements in the figure appeared to maintain their relative positions as the figure moved. Ratings of coherence for both dot and line patterns were found to increase with the number of elements in the pattern. Coherence was judged greatest for patterns rotating about a vertical axis and least for patterns rotating about an axis at an angle of 45° from the vertical and 45° from the plane of the display. Intermediate coherence judgments were obtained with the tumbling patterns. Ratings were higher for a given number of line segments than for the same number of dots, and were greater for connected line segments than for unconnected ones. (The connected line segments produced figures similar in appearance to the wire figures studied by Wallach and O'Connell.) Many of the subjects in these experiments reported seeing every display in three dimensions, although the highest coherence rating was applied to the displays less than half the time. This indicated that the projection of a pattern undergoing a rigid transformation in three-dimensional space can, at the same time, be perceived as three-dimensional and nonrigid. This was the case for most of the figures Green studied. The perception of a rigid three-dimensional object cannot be equated with the perception of motion in depth.

FIGURE 4.10.   Types of patterns studied by Green (1961).

Braunstein (1962) used Green's method in two experiments that examined depth (Experiment 1) and coherence (Experiment 2) judgments for displays of 2, 3, 4, 5, or 6 dots rotating about a vertical axis. The displays were produced with one of three polar projections (Figure 4.11a) or with a parallel projection (Figure 4.11b). The dots were randomly positioned in an imaginary cube, having a side of two arbitrary units. The four projections were produced by varying the computed distance between the projection point and the space in which the dots were located. The projection point was located at 2, 4, 16, or 512 units from the center of the cube. (The 512-unit distance yielded a parallel projection because it produced no perspective changes within the physical resolution of the display.) A perspective ratio was defined as a measure of these variations in the distance of the projection point. The ratio is obtained by dividing the sum of the projection point distance and half the extent in depth of the pattern, by the difference between that distance and half that extent. This definition is illustrated in Figure 4.12. The ratio is a measure of the maximum possible change that can occur in the projection of a distance within the three-dimensional pattern. If two dots, for example, were located on one of the X–Y planes of the imaginary cube, the ratio of their projected separation when that X–Y plane was closest to the projection point, to their projected separation when that plane was most distant from the projection point would be the perspective ratio. For the 2-unit cube in this experiment, the projection point distances of 2, 4, 16 and 512 yielded perspective ratios of 3.00, 1.67, 1.13 and 1.00, respectively. A ratio of exactly 1.0 represents a parallel projection. (The ratio in Green's 1961 experiments was constant at 1.11).

The subject viewed the displays monocularly through a tube that limited his field of view to a circular area within the projection screen (Figure 4.13). The displays were presented in pairs and the subject was

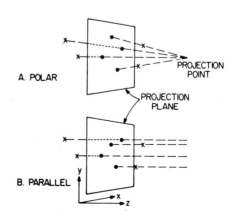

FIGURE 4.11. Comparison of polar and parallel projections. [After Braunstein, 1966.]

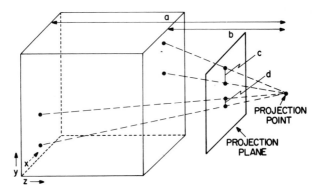

FIGURE 4.12. The perspective ratio for projections of points on a cube. Perspective is defined as a/b, or equivalently, c/d. [After Braunstein, 1962.]

required to indicate which member of each pair appeared more three-dimensional (Experiment 1) or more coherent (Experiment 2). Figure 4.14 shows the results for number of dots. Judged three-dimensionality increased steadily with numerosity. Coherence judgments dropped between the two- and three-dot conditions and remained relatively stable between the three- and six-dot conditions. The high coherence ratings for two-dot pattern is not surprising. Any transformation of a two-dot pattern could be a projection of the end points of a rigid rod moving in three-dimensional space. The increased coherence judgments that Green found with increasing numerosity did not occur in the overall results. This was probably due to the smaller number of dots and higher perspective levels used in Braunstein's study. (There was an indication of increasing coherence with increasing numerosity for the three highest levels—4, 5, and 6 dots—at the 1.13 perspective level.)

The results for perspective variations (Figure 4.15) show a striking contrast between the effects of this variable on depth judgments and its effect on coherence judgments: The effects are exactly opposite. Judged depth was greater for the higher perspective displays, but thse displays

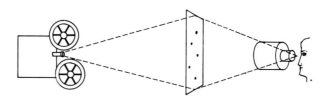

FIGURE 4.13. Viewing arrangement used by Braunstein (1962).

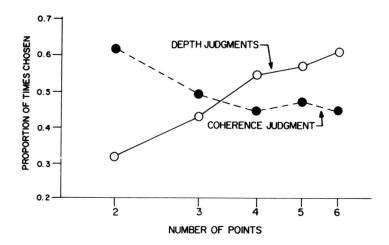

FIGURE 4.14. Effect of numerosity on depth and coherence judgments. [After Braunstein, 1962.]

appeared less rigid. This finding was consistent with Green's (1961) conclusion that the perception of depth in a transforming pattern does not necessarily result in the perception of a rigid configuration.

Braunstein (1966) used a similar method of producing stimulus displays and a similar viewing arrangement in a further study of the effects of perspective on perceived depth. Dots randomly arranged within the confines of an unseen sphere were shown rotating about either a horizontal or a vertical axis. Each transformation was displayed with both a parallel and a polar projection. All of the 24 subjects indicated that they saw a three-dimensional pattern for the parallel projections of rotation about both axes and for the polar projection of rotation about the X axis, and all but two made this response to the polar projection of rotation about the Y axis. Perspective variations did not affect the tendency to perceive the pattern as three-dimensional, though these variations did affect the accuracy of judgments of direction of rotation. This is a further indication that separate processes are involved in depth and direction judgments. We will return to this aspect of the study in Chapter 6.

SYSTEMATIC VARIATIONS IN THE PROJECTION PLANE

The computer animation technique has been used in specific tests of the Wallach and O'Connell hypothesis that contours simultaneously changing in length and direction are necessary and sufficient for the perception of depth in transforming two-dimensional patterns. Johansson and Jansson

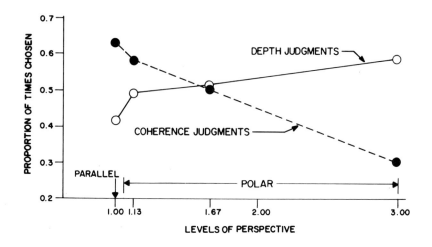

FIGURE 4.15. Effect of perspective on depth and coherence judgments. [After Braunstein, 1962.]

(1968) displayed motion picture sequences of a single line segment that changed in length only, in direction only, or in both length and direction. The projection screen was viewed binocularly from a distance of 8 m. The room was sufficiently dark so that the line appeared to be a "luminous object moving in a dark space (Johansson & Jansson, 1968, p. 168)." All verbal reports for displays in which the line simultaneously changed in length and direction were of three-dimensional perceptions. When the line changed in direction only, about half the reports were of two-dimensional perceptions and half of three-dimensional perceptions. For changes in length only, about two-thirds of the reports were of three-dimensional perceptions. More than 90% of the three-dimensional reports for all stimuli were of a line of constant length rotating in depth about a fixed point. Like White and Mueser, Johansson and Jansson found a much higher percentage of depth reports for changes in length alone or in direction alone than did Wallach and O'Connell. Again, this was probably due to a combination of factors, memory effects occurring within the sequence of trials and reduced indications of flatness in the viewing situation. Stimulus displays with single changes and combined changes were presented repeatedly in a random order, so that most single changes occurred after the subject had seen one or more combined length and direction changes. The viewing distance reduced flatness indications from accommodation and binocular disparity, and the darkness of the room concealed the borders and texture of the screen.

Two studies by Börjesson and von Hofsten (1972, 1973) systematically considered the relationships between projection plane motions in two-dot and three-dot patterns and the perception of rotary and translatory motions in depth. The two-dot stimuli were drawn from a factorial combination of three levels of common motion and three levels of relative motion. Common motion was defined as identical simultaneous translations of both dots in the frontal plane. The three levels of common motion were: no common motion, horizontal common motion, and vertical common motion. The column headings in Figure 4.16 illustrate these motions. The relative motions were defined as horizontal translations of the two dots in the frontal plane that were equal in magnitude but opposite in direction. The three levels of relative motion were: no relative motion, concurrent relative motion (dots moving toward a common point), and nonconcurrent relative motion (dots moving along parallel paths, toward a common line). The relative motions are shown in the row headings in Figure 4.16. The combined motions, shown in the cells of Figure 4.16, were presented to subjects by means of computer controlled displays. The displays were viewed binocularly through an optical device that focused the image at infinity, minimizing flatness indications

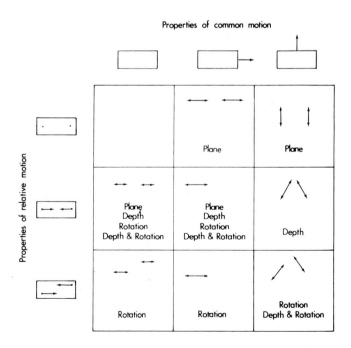

FIGURE 4.16. Main perceptual reports evoked by two-dot motions. [After Börjesson & von Hofsten, 1972.]

based on accommodation. Each dot moved back and forth in its path at a constant velocity. The dots disappeared from view at each end of their paths before changing direction.

The dominant perceptual reports are shown in Figure 4.16. Rotary motion in depth, about an oblique axis, was dominant whenever there was nonconcurrent relative motion. The dots in these displays were often described as representing the endpoints of a rod rotating in depth. This seems to support earlier findings that a contour, or in this case an imaginary line between two dots, must change simultaneously in length and direction in order to elicit reports of rotation in depth. With concurrent relative motions, the change in an imaginary line connecting the dots was in length only. There is, however, another factor that may be related to the tendency to perceive only the nonconcurrent relative motions as representing rotary motions in depth. The rate of change in the distance between the dots was nonlinear for nonconcurrent motions, but was linear for concurrent motions. A perceptual process that produced judgments of motion on a plane with linear changes in the separations of pattern elements, and produced judgments of rotary motion in depth for nonlinear changes could account for the difference in results between concurrent and nonconcurrent motions. Such a process appears likely, although the evidence is inconclusive.

Translatory motions in depth (translations along the Z axis) were the dominant report when a concurrent horizontal motion was combined with a common vertical motion (Figure 4.16, Cell 6). (This finding will be discussed in a later section.) Reports of motion in depth also occurred in two other cells of Figure 4.16 but were not dominant, indicating ambiguity in the available information. Detailed studies involving cells 4, 6, 7, and 9 in Figure 4.16 provided the following quantitative results: "The greater the common motion, the greater is the number of reported translatory motions in depth, and the greater the vertical separation of the relative motion paths, the greater is the number of reported rotations in depth [1972, p. 267]."

In a series of experiments extending their research to three-dot patterns, Börjesson and von Hofsten (1973) reached the following conclusions: (1) Depth relationships are ambiguous for dots that move back and forth along a single straight line (Figure 4.17a). (This conclusion was based on observations of dots moving at linear velocities in the frontal plane.) (2) For patterns that vary in two dimensions on the projection plane: (a) Concurrent relative motions (dots moving toward a common point on the projection plane) are perceived as translations in depth (Figure 4.17b). (b) Parallel relative motions (relative motions toward a common line on the projection plane) are perceived as rotary motions in

FIGURE 4.17. Examples of (a) three dots moving in parallel paths, (b) concurrent relative motions of three dots, (c) parallel relative motions of three dots, and (d) combinations of concurrent and parallel relative motions. [After Börjesson & von Hofsten, 1973.]

depth (Figure 4.17c). (c) Algebraic combinations of concurrent and parallel relative motions may be perceived as combined translations and rotations in depth, provided that these motions are in phase, i.e., that motions toward the common point and toward the common line are coordinated (Figure 4.17d). When the combined motions were out of phase, most reports were of patterns simultaneously rotating in depth and changing in shape.

CONCLUSIONS: ROTATION ABOUT THE X OR Y AXIS

The experiments summarized in this section lead to the following conclusions about the conditions under which a changing image on a projection plane is perceived as a rotary motion in depth:

1. There are no special conditions required for the perception of a transformation as occurring in three-dimensional space. A two-dimensional perception is more likely only when there are specific indications of flatness: a visible border around the projection screen, effective binocular vision without disparity, a visible uniform texture on the screen, or uniform velocities displayed by moving pattern elements.

2. Conditions can be identified that increase the likelihood of depth perception, especially when conflicting indications of flatness are present:

a. The simultaneous change in length and direction of a projected contour is the best supported and probably the most important such condition.

b. Perspective factors, such as the convergence of horizontal contours at the same time as the compression of vertical contours (e.g., a rectangle becoming a trapezoid) appear to increase depth reports. These factors usually include a simultaneous change in the length and direction of contours. It is uncertain whether an accurate perspective representation contributes more to perceived depth than any other simultaneous length and direction change.

c. Nonlinear length changes may be more effective than linear ones, although the evidence is inconclusive. (The waveform of direction changes did not seem to be important in a pilot study by Johansson and Jansson, 1967).

3. The likelihood of depth perception is not closely tied to the perception of a rigid object or configuration, and across some variables (e.g., perspective) these perceptions are inversely related.

Rotations about the Z Axis

The stereokinetic effect described in Chapter 2 occurs when certain two-dimensional geometric patterns are rotated in the frontal plane. Wallach, Weisz, and Adams (1956) conducted detailed studies with two patterns, seeking to discover a relationship between the stereokinetic effect and the kinetic depth effect. The first pattern was a white ellipse pasted onto a black cardboard disc (Figure 4.18a). The disc was located six inches above the floor and was rotated at 20 rpm. The subjects observed it from a standing position. After 30 sec of binocular observation and 10–60 sec of monocular observation, if a subject had failed to report observing a circular disc rolling around on its edge, this possibility was suggested. None of the 47 subjects reported the three-dimensional

a   b

FIGURE 4.18.   (a) The rotating ellipse, and (b) the six overlapping rings. [After Wallach, Weisz, & Adams, 1956.]

effect during binocular observation; 6 reported seeing the tilted disc during monocular observation, without suggestion; 34 reported seeing it only after suggestion; 7 reported never seeing it. Most of the subjects who reported seeing the tilted disc gave consistent descriptions of aspects of the apparent disc not described by the experimenter, such as slant changes, indicating that they were not merely repeating the experimenter's suggestions. The failure of the depth effect to occur with binocular observation and its weakness under monocular conditions were taken as evidence that this instance of the stereokinetic effect was not comparable to the kinetic depth effect.

The second pattern studied by Wallach, Weisz, and Adams consisted of six overlapping circles (Figure 4.18b). The same observation procedure was used. Of the 12 naive subjects, 10 reported seeing the figure as three-dimensional during binocular observation of its rotation, one reported it as such during monocular observation, and one required suggestion. The three-dimensional form was described as resembling a bedspring. The effect obtained with this figure, because of its regular and spontaneous occurrence, was held to resemble the kinetic depth effect. Wallach, Weisz, and Adams then posed the question of whether these rotating figures present imaginary lines to the observer that vary in length and direction. Imaginary lines connecting actual parts of the figures did not undergo any changes during rotation, but there may have been imaginary lines connecting *perceived* parts of the figures that simultaneously changed in length and direction. Figure 4.19 shows two circles before and after a 90° rotation about the Z axis. There is, of course, no change in the projected spacing of any parts of these circles. If, however, the subject perceives the inner circle as moving down and to the right as the outer circle remains stationary, there is a line connecting perceived parts of the circles that changes in length and direction.

Fischer (1956) examined the effects of five factors on the stereokinetic effect: (*a*) the extent to which the circles overlapped (offset); (*b*) the location of the circles on the turntable (placement); (*c*) equal versus un-

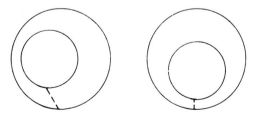

FIGURE 4.19. Length and direction changes for an imaginary line connecting parts of two rotating circles. [After Wallach, Weisz, & Adams, 1956.]

equal circle diameters; (d) monocular versus binocular viewing; and (e) clockwise versus counterclockwise rotation. Offset varied from concentric to tangential. Placement had three levels: The circles were located at the center of the turntable; they were located peripherally so that the axis connecting the circles was located on a radius of the circle, or they were located peripherally with the axis connecting the circles perpendicular to a radius. Examples of Fischer's stimuli are shown in Figure 4.20. Subjects were asked to estimate amount of depth perceived by adjusting a sliding gauge. Offset was the principal determinant of judged depth. Figures in which the circles were concentric or tangential were judged to be flat. Within these limits, judged depth increased with increasing distance between the centers of the rotating circles. Judged depth was greater with monocular viewing. The effects of placement, equality of diameters and direction of rotation were not significant. There was an effect of placement, however, on judgments of the relative depth of the two circles. When the circles were placed at different distances from the center of the turntable, the outer circle was judged closer 92% of the time. This circle had a greater linear velocity. Fischer concluded that subjects organized the rotating offset circles into three-dimensional objects on the basis of their past experience with rotating objects, the equal circles suggesting cylinders and the unequal circles suggesting cones. There is, however, no direct evidence that the stereokinetic effect is related to past experience with rotating objects. The increase in judged depth with monocular viewing was recognized as the possible result of the elimination of lack of disparity as a flatness cue.

Rotation about the Z axis was included in the study by Braunstein (1966) described in the preceding section. The stimuli were random dot patterns, the dots located either on a circle or confined to an imaginary

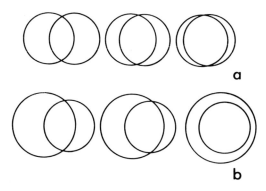

FIGURE 4.20. Stimulus figures showing variations in offset for (a) equal, and (b) unequal diameters. [After Fischer, 1956.]

sphere. The spherical arrangement was displayed with either a polar or a parallel projection. Each of the three displays (two-dimensional, three-dimensional parallel, and three-dimensional polar) was judged to appear three-dimensional by about half (44%, 53%, and 50%, respectively) of the subjects. This result is a further reflection of the ambiguity of the information provided by this transformation.

In general, depth perception in patterns rotating about the Z axis has received less attention than depth perception resulting from other transformations. Our understanding of the stereokinetic effect remains far from complete; however, there is sufficient information in the studies cited to suggest the following tentative conclusions:

1. The process of rotation alone, regardless of the figure, enhances depth perception. This is probably because rotation decreases indications of the flatness of the surface on which the figure is drawn by making the surface texture less visible. Mefferd and Wieland (1967) found increased instances of perceived depth during rotation with a variety of figures, apparently for this reason.

2. The three-dimensional perceptions obtained with certain figures, specifically circles and ellipses, are based on a two-stage process:

a. In the first stage, the figure is not perceived as rotating with the turntable. A circle at the center of the turntable will appear stationary (Wallach, Weisz, & Adams, 1956). Other figures, such as overlapping rings, will appear to undergo changes in orientation rather than complete rotation. Parts of the figure will appear to change their relative orientations and their relative velocities during rotation. Figures lacking easily determinable orientations, like circles, will retain their shapes and others, like ellipses, will appear to distort during rotation.

b. In the second stage, which occurs later and less reliably than the first stage, the nonveridical perceptions of change in relative orientation and relative velocity of parts of the figure are converted to the perception of a rigid three-dimensional object rotating in depth. The perceived axis of rotation appears to be at an angle to the line of sight (the Z axis) and to itself be rotating about that axis.

Exactly how depth perception comes about in the second stage is uncertain. It seems to be related to the *apparent* variations in the relative positions of parts of the pattern that occur as a result of the nonveridical perceptions in the first stage. A vector analysis (Börjesson & von Hofsten, 1972, 1973), based not on actual motions in the frontal plane but on motions perceived in the first stage, might be enlightening.

Translations along the X and Y Axes

The classical depth cue of motion parallax is a special case of translation along the X axis. It usually has been defined in terms of two velocities on the projection plane, the greater velocity implying a closer object. In direct vision there is usually a gradient of velocities available during translations of objects along paths perpendicular to the line of sight, rather than merely two velocities (Gibson, 1946). The question of whether there is a qualitative difference in depth judgments for the two-velocity and velocity gradient cases was considered by Gibson, Gibson, Smith, and Flock (1959). A shadow projection device was used, with the eye and point light source equidistant from the screen. In one experiment, the shadow casters were patterns affixed to two transparent mounts (Figure 4.21a). An opaque paper circle was pasted on each mount in one condition. In another condition, a random texture (obtained by sprinkling talcum powder) was produced on each mount. The shadow casters were translated horizontally at the same rate. The relative velocities projected by the two shadow casters were varied by varying their distances from the point source. Each subject first observed a motionless display, then observed the patterns in motion at a maximum velocity difference (a ratio of the slower to faster velocities of .51), and finally observed the patterns in motion at a minimum velocity difference (a .97 ratio). The subject was asked to describe what he saw in the window. All subjects reported the motionless textures to be without differences in depth, but·4 of the 26 subjects reported the two motionless circles to be at different distances. At the maximum velocity difference, all subjects reported the textures to be two surfaces separated in depth and 22 of the 26 subjects reported the two spots to be separated in depth. There were no reports of separation in depth for the two textures at the minimum velocity difference. Of the 26 subjects, 7 reported separation in depth for the spots at the minimum difference. There was some ambiguity in the direction of apparent depth, even at the greater velocity difference. Nearly one-quarter of the subjects judged that the slower velocity represented a nearer surface. There were spontaneous reversals of the front–back relationship. Gibson et al. concluded from these results that the two-velocity display did not result in a perception of depth in the usual sense, but only in a separation of one surface into two.

In a second experiment, the shadow caster was a transparent sheet on which paint had been spattered. The top of the shadow caster was slanted away from the point source at a 45° angle (Figure 4.21b). All subjects saw the display of the shadow caster undergoing an X translation. One group saw it in motion only; another group first saw it stationary and

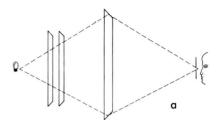

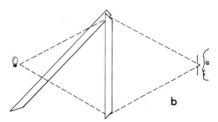

FIGURE 4.21. The shadow projection device (a) with two parallel mounts, and (b) with one slanted mount. [After Gibson, Gibson, Smith, and Flock, 1959.]

then in motion. The stationary display was never reported to be slanted backward into space. When the surface was in motion, 45 of the 49 subjects reported perceptions of a receding surface. The overall conclusion of Gibson *et al.* was that there are two kinds of depth experience: "empty" depth in which one surface may be seen in front of another, as in their first experiment; and "filled" depth, based on a receding surface, as in their second experiment.

The Gibson *et al.* (1959) experiments used polar projections of the translating patterns. The perception of depth in patterns rotating about the X or Y axis does not depend on whether a parallel or a polar projection is displayed, but the situation is quite different for patterns translating along these axes. Braunstein (1966) found the type of projection to be critical for three-dimensional patterns translating along these axes. The study included both two- and three-dimensional patterns translating along the X or Y axes. In the two-dimensional pattern, dots were randomly arranged on the surface of a frontally oriented plane. The dots were randomly arranged within the confines of an imaginary cylinder in the three-dimensional pattern. The long axis of the cylinder was coincident with the axis of translation. Both the plane and the cylinder were sufficiently long so that edges did not appear in the display during the translation process. The three-dimensional pattern was displayed with either a polar or a parallel projection. (Type of projection was not relevant for the two-dimensional pattern, because this pattern lacked differential depth.) The three types of displays — two-dimensional, three-dimensional with a parallel projection, and three-dimensional with a polar projection — were judged to appear three-dimensional by 31%, 44%, and 91% of the subjects, respectively, for the X translation, and by 9%, 38%, and 94% of the subjects, respectively, for the Y translation. Both the two-dimensional pattern and the parallel projection of the three-dimensional pattern displayed dots moving at a uniform velocity. The displays differed in texture, however, in that the two-dimensional pattern projected a uniform texture and the three-dimensional pattern projected an increasingly dense texture toward the vertical (in the X translation) or horizontal (in the Y translation) center of the projection. This texture gradient was due to the cylindrical shape of the volume in which the dots were located in three-dimensional space. The third display type, three-dimensional with a polar projection, combined the texture gradient just described with a corresponding velocity gradient and was judged three-dimensional by almost all subjects. This study showed effects of both the texture and velocity gradients on judgments of depth in random dot patterns translating along the X or Y axis. When both gradients were uniform, two-dimensional reports predominated. When the velocity gradient was uniform but the texture gradient was not, depth was ambiguous. When both gradients indicated variations in depth, almost all reports were of three-dimensional perceptions.

The problem of separating the effects of velocity and texture gradients is clearly of importance to the determination of the role of velocity gradients in depth perception for patterns translating along the X or Y axes. This problem had been considered previously by Gibson and Carel (1952). They posed the question of whether a gradient of velocities was sufficient to produce an impression of a receding surface. Each velocity, they noted, must be carried by an element of a pattern. There cannot be a velocity gradient without a texture density gradient. Even the use of a uniform texture would not allow the experimenter to produce a velocity gradient in isolation. A uniform texture would indicate a frontally oriented surface. This would provide conflicting information to the observer, if the velocity gradient indicated a receding surface. Gibson and Carel concluded that a velocity gradient cannot be produced in isolation. It must either correspond to or be in opposition to a texture density gradient. They decided to study the perception of a uniform texture density gradient combined with a velocity gradient in which element velocity was proportional to its distance from the top of the display. The device used to produce this effect was a 6-foot (1.83 m) disc covered with narrow line segments of luminous paint radiating from its center. The lines were visible only through horizontal slits arranged in a triangle at the bottom of a screen covering the disc. Of 10 naive subjects, only

3 reported perceiving a receding plane on the basis of this display. Gibson and Carel concluded that the simulation of a receding surface produced by their device was probably inadequate. The device displayed only small spots of light separated by large areas of darkness, and lacked the phenomenal "hardness" or "impenetrability" of a rigid surface. They also concluded that the incompatible texture gradient contributed to the ambiguity of the depth that might have been implied by the velocity gradient, but this conclusion is questionable, for if their simulation was inadequate, there was really no way to assess the influence of conflicting gradients.

The problem of separating the effects of texture and velocity gradients was considered more recently by Braunstein (1968). Through the use of computer animation techniques, it was possible to generate accurate projections of the texture gradients and velocity gradients that would be produced during the translation of slanted surfaces and to display conflicts in these gradients that would be impossible in direct vision. In computer animation, the position of each dot on each frame of a motion picture can be determined independently. It is a straightforward matter to position the dots on a frame in accordance with one slant angle and to determine the amount each dot is to move from frame to frame in accordance with a different slant angle.

Displays were produced representing polar projections of dots randomly distributed over the surface of a plane. The plane was either perpendicular to the line of sight, a slant of $0°$, or slanted away from the observer at the top or bottom. It was either translated horizontally or was stationary. Four slant angles ($0°$, $20°$, $40°$, $60°$) were used in computing the texture density gradients. The same four angles were used in computing the velocity gradients. Only when the texture and velocity angles were equal did the gradients correspond, as they would in normal vision. In all other cases, except for the stationary displays of each texture gradient, the two gradients provided conflicting indications of slant. Consider, for example, a display produced with a texture gradient based on a $60°$ slant and a velocity gradient based on a $0°$ slant (Figure 4.22a). Each individual frame of the motion picture would show a texture gradient increasing in density toward the top of the display. The dots, however, all would move across the projection screen at the same velocity. To turn the example around, consider a display produced with a texture gradient of $0°$ and a velocity gradient of $60°$ (Figure 4.22b). The texture would be uniform, but the dots would move across the screen at varying velocities, those nearest the top moving most slowly and those nearest the bottom moving most rapidly.

The subjects observed 10-sec motion picture sequences of planes trans-

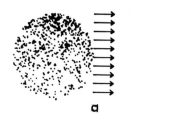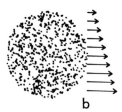

FIGURE 4.22.   (a) A 60° texture gradient combined with a 0° velocity gradient, and (b) a 0° texture gradient combined with a 60° velocity gradient.

lating along the X axis and displaying each of the 16 combinations of texture and velocity gradients. Four additional sequences displayed stationary textures at each level of texture gradient. The results dealing with accuracy of slant judgments for the various combinations of gradients will be discussed in a later chapter.   Of interest here are the factors affecting whether the plane was judged to be frontally oriented or to be receding in depth. The comparison relevant to this question is that of stationary displays with those displays moving at a uniform velocity (i.e., a velocity gradient based on a slant of 0°). The mean slant judgments for stationary displays with texture gradients based on angles of 0°, 20°, 40°, and 60° were −.3°, 2.1°, 1.8°, and 11.6°, respectively. When the same texture gradients were displayed translating at a uniform velocity, the mean slant judgments were 1.7°, −.2°, .2°, and 2.4°. The reduction in judged slant with uniform velocity, especially at the most extreme texture gradient, demonstrates that uniform velocity is an indicator of flatness. This is true even when the texture gradient would otherwise indicate a surface receding in depth.

Uniform texture seems to reduce apparent slant when the velocity gradient is held constant. With a uniform texture (based on a slant of 0°), the judged slants for velocity gradients of 20°, 40°, and 60° were 11.7°, 18.6°, and 20.7°. This can be contrasted to judgments of 27.8°, 34.8°, and 41.5° for the same three velocity gradients, but with a 60° texture gradient. Uniform gradients indicate a flat surface, while gradients decreasing toward the top or bottom of the display indicate a slanted surface. Velocity gradients are more effective than texture gradients in determining whether a surface is perceived as being in the frontal plane or slanted in depth.

The studies in this section were concerned with three questions about the perception of depth in patterns translating along the X or Y axis: (1) Is there a qualitative difference between the perception of two projected velocities and the perception of a gradient of velocities? (2) Does the type of projection (polar versus parallel) affect the likelihood that depth will be perceived? (3) Are velocity gradients more effective than texture gradients in determining whether depth will be perceived? There is strong evidence supporting answers of "yes" to the second and third questions. The perception of depth in three-dimensional patterns undergoing translations along the X or Y axis is strongly dependent on the use of polar projections. Velocity gradients are markedly more effective than texture gradients in determining perceived depth, when these two sources of information are placed in conflict. The answer to the first question is not as clear. The finding of ambiguity in the direction of apparent depth in the two-velocity case by Gibson *et al.* (1959) is not a sufficient basis for calling this "empty" depth in contrast to the "filled" depth associated with a gradient of velocities. There are many instances of ambiguous depth relationships for objects that appear to have continuous extent in depth. The distant windmill and most of the kinetic depth figures are examples. Ambiguity of front–back relationships was also found in informal reports of people who observed polar projections of dots randomly arranged in a translating cylinder (Braunstein, 1966). These findings may reflect an inherent ambiguity in polar projections of random textures translating along the X or Y axis. Dots traveling at varying velocities across the projection plane could, geometrically, represent one of three situations in three-dimensional space: (1) The dots could be located at varying distances from the observer and be moving at the same velocities; (2) the dots could be located at the same distance from the observer and be moving at varying velocities; or (3) the dots could be located at varying distances and be moving at varying velocities. The first perception appears to be dominant when the velocities of the projected dots are proportional to their distances from the top of the projection plane. This was the case for the slanted plane in Gibson *et al.*'s (1959) second experiment and for the simulated slanted planes in Braunstein's (1968) experiment. The second perception occurs when the differences in velocity in the display are too small to overcome indications of flatness that may be present in the display. This seems to have been the case for the minimum velocity difference condition in Gibson *et al.*'s (1959) first experiment. The third perception occurs in most other cases, whether there are just two velocities or a range of velocities displayed on the projection plane. The minimum conditions for the perception of depth in the multiple velocity case remain to be explored.

Translations along the Z Axis

Kilpatrick and Ittelson (1951) studied combinations of real and simulated translations along the Z axis using an apparatus that could change the size of a stimulus in a frontal plane, change its distance from the observer, or change both the size and distance in any desired combination. The apparatus was essentially a light box mounted behind a variable diaphragm, which could be moved along tracks parallel to the observer's line of sight. By adusting the correspondence between the size and distance of the stimulus, its projected size could be made to increase as it approached the observer, remain constant as it approached, or even to decrease as it approached. Monocular observers, watching the illuminated stimulus in an otherwise dark room from a distance of at least 6 feet, reported it to be approaching in the first case, motionless in the second, and receding in the third. (The tendency to perceive a projected size change as a distance change has thwarted several attempts to symbolically portray inflation in television commercials by means of a "shrinking" dollar. When the dollar changes in size on the television screen, it appears to be receding rather than shrinking.)

Changes in size and illumination were used by Kilpatrick (1952) to create an impression of translation along the Z axis in the well-known balloon demonstration. An apparatus was used that could independently vary the relative size and illumination of two balloons. The illuminated balloons, observed at a distance of 10 feet in an otherwise dark room, were reported to have the appearance of two spheres. When the balloons were equal in size and illumination, they were judged equal in distance. When the size of one balloon was increased relative to the other and the illuminations were kept equal, the balloon that was increasing in size appeared to be approaching. When the illumination of one balloon was increased and the sizes were held constant, the balloon increasing in illumination was reported as approaching, but to a lesser degree than with size changes. Size was dominant when the two changes indicated conflicting depth.

Expanding textures in the projection plane, like expanding projections of objects, are perceived as translating along the Z axis. Braunstein (1966) studied these translations for two random dot patterns, dots confined to a circle perpendicular to the line of sight and dots confined to a sphere, with the line of sight passing through its origin. As in the other parts of that study, the projected size and shape of each dot remained constant during translation. Only the projected distances between the dots were varied. The dot pattern always filled the viewing area so that no contour was visible. The translations were displayed with either a parallel or a polar projection. There were no changes in the positions of the projected dots in the parallel projections. While the dots were theoretically moving toward or away from the observer, they were always infinitely distant. Reports of perceived depth in the parallel projections were obtained from 22% and 59% of the subjects for the two-dimensional and three-dimensional patterns, respectively. This difference is attributable to the difference in the texture gradients projected by the two patterns (Figure 4.23), because no motion was visible. In polar projections, reports of perceived depth were obtained from 38% and 88% of the subjects, respectively, for the two textures. The question asked of the subjects was whether the pattern was three-dimensional, not whether it was moving in depth. Preliminary studies indicated that the polar projections of both patterns appeared to be moving in depth for all subjects. Increasing or decreasing the separation of nonvarying texture elements appears to be sufficient to elicit reports of an approaching or receding pattern. Subjects can, at the same time, distinguish between two- and three-dimensional textures, apparently on the basis of differential rates of increase or decrease in the spacing of the elements.

In the experiments previously described, Börjesson and von Hofsten (1972, 1973) obtained reports of translations along the Z axis with patterns containing only two or three nonvarying texture elements. This was the dominant report when the dots in a pattern approached a common point, provided that the paths of the dots were not confined to a single straight line. Geometrically, dots moving toward a common point can represent projections of dots that are receding from the observer while maintaining a fixed separation in three-dimensional space, whether or not the dots remain aligned during the transformation. The difference in the perceptual effects of aligned and nonaligned patterns is therefore of particular interest. In both cases, each dot moved along its path at a constant rate. A line connecting the two dots would have changed in length only, and the rate of this change would have been constant in both cases. In an accurate polar projection of two dots receding at a constant velocity, the rate of change in the projected separation of the dots would decrease as the dots receded. This rate of change did not occur in either the aligned

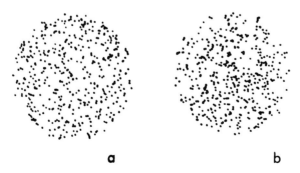

a   b

FIGURE 4.23.   Parallel projections of dots (a) confined to a circle, and (b) confined to a sphere.

or nonaligned patterns. In the nonaligned patterns, the converging paths of the dots may have implied recession in depth, just as converging lines in a static scene tend to be registered as the contours of a receding surface. Converging lines are an especially effective indicator of depth. In the static case, a receding surface can be suggested by converging lines even when these lines are drawn on an obviously flat surface. This is, at least in part, the basis of the Ponzo illusion (Gregory, 1964). In the dynamic case, converging linear paths may imply recession in depth even when the dots moving along these paths are traveling at constant velocities. When the dots in the Börjesson and von Hofsten experiments were aligned, the display lacked converging linear paths. The increases and decreases in the separations between dots may have served as indicators of motion in depth in the absence of converging linear paths, but these distance changes apparently could not overcome the flatness indicated by the constant velocities of the dots. Had the dots in the aligned case decelerated as they moved together and accelerated as they separated, the proportion of depth reports might have been higher. There is, at present, very little information on the effects of changes in the projected velocities of pattern elements. Velocity changes are probably more important in the perception of rotations than in the perception of translations. The perception of rotations seems to depend on the occurrence of motions on the projection plane that approximate projections of patterns moving at constant angular velocities in three-dimensional space. Perspective is not critical; rotation in depth is reported in parallel as well as polar projections. In contrast, depth is reliably reported only in polar projections of translations. The effects of perspective, such as the appearance of converging linear paths in the projection plane, is critical to the perception of translations in depth.

In general, overall size changes are perceived as representing translations along the Z axis, in the absence of conflicting indications of flatness in the display. This holds for projections of objects that shrink or expand, as well as for texture elements that approach or recede from a common point. The texture elements do not have to decelerate as they approach the common point or accelerate as they recede from it, as they would in actual polar projections of rigid patterns, in order for translations in depth to be perceived. If the elements of two-dot or three-dot patterns move along common lines at constant velocities on the projection plane, however, they tend to be perceived as representing motion in the frontal plane. It is not yet known whether such aligned patterns would be perceived as representing translations in depth if the dots accelerated as they moved apart and decelerated as they came together. The ability of subjects to distinguish between two-dimensional and three-dimensional random dot patterns on the basis of translations along the Z axis (Braunstein, 1966) does suggest such a sensitivity to variations in the acceleration of projected texture elements.

Conclusion

An overall conclusion that can be drawn from this research is that accurate polar projections of rigid motions in three-dimensional space almost invariably elicit reports of perceived depth, even in the presence of conflicting indications of flatness. The one exception is rotation about the Z axis. This appears to be an inherently ambiguous transformation that cannot overcome conflicting flatness indications in the display or in the viewing conditions. In the case of rotation about the X or Y axis, parallel projections as well as polar projections reliably elicit reports of perceived rotary motion in depth. Though projections of rigid motions elicit reports of depth, reports of perceived depth are not necessarily accompanied by reports of rigid motions. Reports of elastic motions in depth are found to varying degrees in most studies using shadow projections or computer animation to simulate rigid motions. These reports are especially prevalent when motions are produced in the frontal plane that have some characteristics of rigid motions in depth but are not accurate simulations of rigid motions. Some of the stimulus displays of Börjesson and von Hofsten (1973), for example, combined motion paths in the projection plane that simulated rotary and translatory motions in depth, but were out of phase. Most reports were of elastic motions in depth.

There are two contrasting explanations of these reports of elastic motions in depth. One explanation holds that the perception of motion in depth on the basis of transformations in the projection plane results from a preference for perceiving an object moving rigidly in three-dimensional space, rather than a distorting two-dimensional pattern. This is assumed to be due to the greater simplicity of the former perception when there is a rigid motion that the two-dimensional projection might represent. When stimulus conditions do not allow for the perception of a totally rigid object, the perception of an object in depth is retained but some perceived elasticity is introduced. The second explanation is that specific perceptions of motion in depth are automatically triggered by certain transformations in the projection plane. Any tendency to perceive a rigid object is secondary. The perceived motion is a direct response to the stimulus information. If it is possible for a rigid pattern to undergo this motion, then rigid motions will be reported; if not, elastic motions will be reported. The view that perceptual processes are applied automatically to motion in the projection plane is the one taken here. The current state of knowledge concerning the relationship between motions in the projection plane and the perception of transformations in three-dimensional space has been described in the various sections of this chapter. Some of the conclusions described in these sections suggest specific processes: One example is Wallach and O'Connell's conclusion that simultaneous length and direction changes are necessary and sufficient for perceived depth.

Another is Börjesson and von Hofsten's conclusion that nonaligned dots converging toward a single point imply a translation along the Z axis. These represent beginnings in the effort to discover the relevant sources of information and the processing rules underlying the perception of depth through motion.

In the concluding section of Chapter 2, some preliminary comments were made about the difficulty of formulating the right questions for research on depth perception. This difficulty is a significant one for much of the research described in this chapter. The question that has been explicit or implicit in most studies is "What transformations must occur in the projection plane in order for motion in depth to be perceived?" This question is traceable to the cue concept of depth perception. It implies the primacy of flatness in visual perception. The primacy of flatness is not supported by the research summarized in this chapter. On the contrary, the overall implication of this research is that depth is likely to be perceived in any dynamic display, even when flatness indications are only partially eliminated. A more appropriate research question would be "What transformations in the projection plane lead to what perceived motions in the external environment?" (Other questions, concerning the accuracy with which relationships in depth are judged, will be considered in the next two chapters.) There are direct implications for the conduct of research on depth perception following from the alternative question proposed here. The principal implication is that indicators of flatness must be carefully controlled if conclusions are to be drawn about the conditions underlying perceived depth. The methods for doing this are straightforward (see Chapter 1). In many of the studies cited in this chapter, these procedures were not fully employed and clear indications of flatness remained in the display or in the viewing conditions. There has been little research on the systematic elimination of indicators of flatness, so it is difficult to estimate the effect that eliminating these indicators might have had on the results of these studies. It is likely that some indicators of flatness could cause even directly viewed three-dimensional scenes to appear two-dimensional.[1]

---

[1] Formal evidence on this question is lacking, though there is some informal support for this hypothesis: People observing three-dimensional recreations of famous paintings at the Laguna Beach, Ca., Pageant of the Masters have reported a marked decrease in perceived depth when a large frame is moved in front of the three-dimensional scene.

5

Slant Perception

THERE ARE MANY LEVELS AT which the three-dimensional world can be meaningfully described. At one level of description, we might consider variations in the luminance of arbitrarily small areas. At another level, we might limit our descriptions to separate recognizable objects. There is an intermediate level which seems to be uniquely important in the study of depth perception. It is a level at which depth relationships are fully or almost fully described, but one at which specific objects need not be recognized, or even present. This is the level of description at which the environment is treated as an array of surfaces at various slants, with respect to the observer's line of regard. There has been relatively little research on the role of motion in the perception of surface slant. There is, on the other hand, a considerable literature on the perception of surface slant in static displays. Almost all of the studies of dynamic factors in slant perception are extensions of this research with static displays. Research on static slant perception will be considered in the first part of this chapter. The second part will review research on slant perception in dynamic displays.

Static Slant Perception

THE SHAPE–SLANT INVARIANCE HYPOTHESIS

The study of slant perception has been closely tied to the study of shape perception. This is a result of attempts to correlate judgments of object shape with judgments of slant, as a test of the shape–slant invariance hypothesis.[1] According to this hypothesis, a given retinal projection is perceived as a particular shape at a particular slant. If the projection remains constant but conditions of observation or other experimental variables alter the perceived slant, the perceived shape is held to change accordingly. Similarly, if the perceived shape is directly altered, the perceived slant must also change according to the invariance hypothesis. Figure 5.1 illustrates a simple case of this hypothesis. The trapezoid in this figure, according to the invariance hypothesis, may be seen as either: (a) a trapezoid in the frontal plane, (b) a rectangle with the top slanted away from the observer, (c) a slightly slanted trapezoid, with the actual top and bottom sides closer to equality than are the projections of those sides, or even (d) a trapezoid with a larger top than bottom, with the bottom slanted away from the observer. Whatever the perceived slant, the shape must perceived accordingly; whatever the perceived shape, the appropriate slant must be perceived.

Some have taken the shape–slant invariance hypothesis to mean that explicit judgments of shape and slant should be highly correlated. This is a

FIGURE 5.1. An illustration of the shape–slant invariance hypothesis.

[1] The shape–slant invariance hypothesis was presented by Koffka (1935) as the solution to the problem of shape constancy: Why does an observer perceive approximately the same shape when viewing an object from different angles? This problem arises as a result of the explicit or implicit acceptance of the eye–camera analogy. The retinal shape of an object varies with the object's slant; the perceived shape often does not. A total acceptance of the analogy requires the explanation of such discrepancies between perception and the retinal image.

naive interpretation of the hypothesis. The use of information about the orientation of a surface by an observer in a shape judgment does not mean that the observer can directly access this information when called upon to make a slant judgment. Different perceptual judgments may use different sources of information and different processing rules, and these judgments may not even be logically consistent. Modern writers have adopted the term "registered" to refer to information used in a perceptual judgment that may not be directly accessible to the observer. For example, one of two objects projecting the same retinal images may be judged larger because the registered distance of that object is greater; but if an explicit distance judgment is required, it may be judged closer because it appears larger. This combination of judgments, though it appears to defy the rules of logic, is not unusual in visual perception. The moon illusion has been convincingly explained in this manner (see Chapter 7).

In order to determine the degree of correlation between shape judgments and slant judgments it was necessary for researchers to produce conditions under which these judgments would vary with a constant retinal projection. This was the motivation for some of the studies of variables affecting slant judgments to be discussed in the following sections. Our concern here will be with factors underlying judged slant. (For reviews of research directly concerned with shape–slant invariance, see Epstein and Park, 1963; Ericksson, 1967.)

TEXTURE GRADIENTS

Most of the empirical research on slant perception was inspired by Gibson's theory "that space-perception is reducible to the perception of visual surfaces [1950a, p. 367]." Gibson recognized that a major research problem associated with this theory was the verification of stimulus correlates for the perception of surface slant. He considered the issue to be the verification rather than the discovery of stimulus correlates, for he had already introduced a series of hypotheses about the nature of these correlates (Gibson, 1946). These hypotheses emphasized the role of texture in slant perception. Specifically, Gibson argued that a texture density gradient was a sufficient stimulus for the perception of surface slant. The line of research he began in order to verify this hypothesis has led to an increasingly detailed analysis of the stimulus correlates underlying slant perception.

The primary question for Gibson's theory was whether a texture density gradient is a sufficient stimulus for the perception of a surface at a slant. Gibson (1950a) attempted to answer this question in a straightforward experiment in which subjects made slant judgments of photographs of slanted surfaces. The photographs were projected onto a translucent screen and observed monocularly through an aperture arrangement that limited the field of view to a circular area within the photograph. The photographs were of two different wallpaper patterns, an irregular pattern and a regular pattern (Figure 5.2), at slants of 10°, 22°, 30° and 45°. Slant judgments correlated well with displayed slant but judged slant was, on the average, about half of the displayed slant. Gibson attributes this discrepancy to indications of the flatness of the projection screen (e.g., lack of differential blur, visibility of the screen's texture). Judged slant was generally greater for the regular than for the irregular texture.

Effects of Texture Regularity. Texture regularity is a broad descriptor that encompasses regularity in the size and shape of texture elements and in their distribution on a surface. Flock and Moscatelli (1964) and Phillips (1970) provide evidence that size and shape regularity is more important than regularity of distribution in determining slant judgments. The Flock and Moscatelli experiment was an extension of Gibson's (1950a) study. Six textures were produced that varied in regularity on three dimensions: element size, element shape, and distribution of elements (Figure 5.3). The textures represented all combinations of regularity and irregularity on these three dimensions except for the omission of textures combining irregularity in size with regularity in distrbution. The textures were observed monocularly at slants of 0°, 10°, 20°, 30° and 40°. Accuracy of slant judgments generally increased with all three dimensions of texture regularity. One exception was that regularity of distribution did not appear to affect slant judgments when the shapes and sizes of the texture elements were regular. Slant judgments for both the most and the least regular textures were more accurate than those found by Gibson (1950a) for his regular and irregular textures, respectively, but there is an important difference in the methods employed in the two studies. Flock and Mos-

FIGURE 5.2. Irregular and regular textures. [From Gibson, 1950a.]

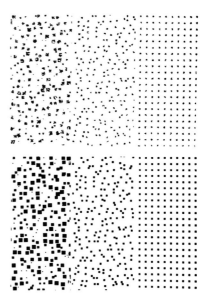

FIGURE 5.3. Six textures varying in regularity. [From Flock & Moscatelli, 1964.]

catelli, unlike Gibson, had their subjects directly observe a slanted surface. The effects of the differential blur and head movements should therefore have reinforced slant indications provided by the texture gradient in the Flock and Moscatelli experiment, rather than contradicted these indications as they might have in Gibson's study. (Another difference, which Flock and Moscatelli point out, is that they used a larger field of view.)

Phillips' (1970) results confirm Flock and Moscatelli's finding that the distribution of the texture elements makes little difference when the elements are uniform in size and shape. Phillips' stimuli were computer generated patterns of ellipses representing circles on a slanted surface. The size and shape each ellipse was determined by one of two slant angles, 45° or 70°. The distribution of ellipses across the displayed pattern was determined by either the same slant angle as the size and shape, or by the other slant angle. A given pattern could therefore represent one slant angle by means of a size and shape gradient and another slant angle by means of a density gradient (Figure 5.4). The patterns were observed monocularly through reduction tubes which limited the field of view to circular areas within each pattern. Relative slant judgments were made for pairs of patterns. In all cases in which the two gradients, size–shape and texture, gave contradictory indications of relative slant, the pattern for which the greater slant was indicated by the size–shape gradient was judged more slanted by at least 11 of the 12 subjects. The density gradient appeared to have a minor effect. The pattern with the density gradient indicating

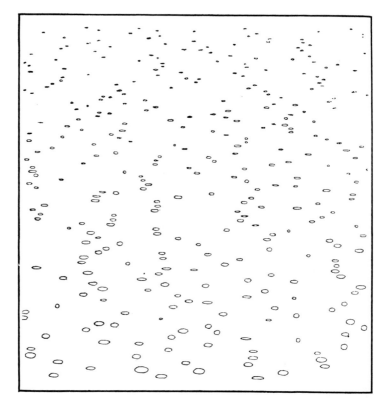

Figure 5.4. A 70° size–shape gradient combined with a 45° density gradient. [From Phillips, 1970.]

greater slant was judged more slanted by most subjects when both patterns displayed the same size–shape gradients.

Effects of Texture Density.   Slant judgments are affected by the density of a texture as well as by its regularity, according to the findings of Gruber and Clark (1956). Subjects judged the slant of a textured surface that had been rotated about a vertical axis. The size of the texture elements, the density of the texture, and the viewing distance were varied. The surface was observed monocularly through an aperture that concealed its borders. Judged slant was considerably below physical slant for all stimulus conditions. Judgments were most accurate with the largest elements, the coarsest texture, and the closest viewing distance, but even these judgments were gross underestimates (12.5°, 18°, and 24.2° for physical slants of 32°, 43°, and 53°, respectively). In a second experiment, an inverted U-shaped function was found relating judged slant to mean distance between texture units. Gruber and Clark concluded that, in order to produce an impression of texture, the elements must be far enough apart not to fuse but not so far apart that they will be seen as separate figures on an untextured ground.

Compression versus Convergence. When a texture is displayed at a slant, its projection shows a general increase in density toward the edge that is slanted away from the subject. This increase in density results from changes in the positions of projected texture elements in both the dimensions of the projection plane as the surface is rotated from the frontal position to the displayed slant. Position changes parallel to the axis of rotation are referred to as convergence of the projected texture, and changes in the perpendicular dimension are referred to as compression. When a random texture is displayed at a slant, there is no direct indication of how the positions of individual texture elements have changed on the projection plane, and consequently no way to assess the relative effects of compression and convergence in producing the density gradient. These effects were potentially separable in the irregular textures studied by Gibson (1950a) and by Flock and Moscattelli (1964) because these textures had identifiable pattern elements. The positions of these elements could be compared when the same irregular texture was displayed at various slants.

Studies of the relative influence of compression and convergence on slant judgments usually have been concerned with regular patterns which clearly separate these two factors. Attneave and Olson (1966) found that when convergence and compression provided conflicting slant indications for a regular grid pattern (Figure 5.5), judged direction of slant was determined by the direction of convergence. Gillam (1968) obtained slant judgments for patterns of lines that were either perpendicular to the axis of rotation, parallel to the axis of rotation, or both perpendicular and parallel (grid patterns). The perpendicular patterns showed only compression when slanted, the parallel patterns showed only convergence, and the grid patterns of course showed both changes. There was little difference in judged slant for the perpendicular (convergence) and grid patterns, but judged slant was significantly lower for the parallel (compression) patterns. Verbal reports obtained in a later study (Gillam, 1970) including only parallel patterns indicated that slant judgments for these patterns were not based on an immediate impression of slant but were intellectual judgments based on a knowledge of perspective. The dominant role of convergence, along with the minor role of compression, has also been found in judgments of direction of rotary motion (see Chapter 6).

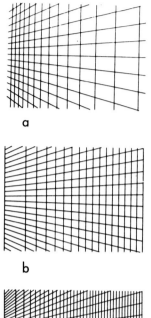

a

b

c

FIGURE 5.5. Linear patterns displaying (a) corresponding compression and convergence information, and (b, c) conflicting compression and convergence information. [From Attneave & Olson, 1966.]

CONTOUR CONVERGENCE

Most of the studies described in the preceding sections used contourless surface textures in order to isolate the effects of texture gradients. Visible surfaces usually have visible contours, and the projections of these contours carry potential information about surface slant. The question of whether contour variations, presented in isolation, serve as an effective stimulus for the perception of surface slant was addressed by Clark, Smith, and Rabe (1955). Subjects were asked to judge the slant of rectangles and trapezoids rotated about a vertical axis. The vertical sides of the trapezoids were parallel, as they would be in the projection of a rectangle rotated about the vertical axis. The midpoints of the vertical sides were at the same height. The forms were painted white and viewed monocularly against a black background. Care was taken to minimize the visibility of both surface and background textures. Slant judgments varied with the projected shape of the figure, regardless of actual shape and physical slant that produced that projection.

Stavrianos (1945) and Freeman (1966a) found slant judgments to vary with the size as well as with the slant of slanted rectangles. Freeman attributed this to a linear perspective effect. He defined perspective alternatively as (a) the slope of the converging lines in the projection of a slanted rectangle and (b) the difference between the projected lengths of the nearer and farther edges. For a rectangle rotated about the X axis, the first variable is determined by both the width of the rectangle and by its slant; the second variable is determined by height, as well as by width and slant. Direct evidence of the relative importance of these two variables in determining slant judgments is not currently available, but there is evidence based on somewhat different stimulus figures indicating that slope is the more effective variable. Braunstein and Payne (1968b), using rectangular grid patterns rotated about the Y axis, found the highest correlation between judged slant and various measures of the projected image to be one of .94, with slope. The correlation of judged slant with measures of the parallel contours was .89, whether the measure used was the difference between the contour lengths, as suggested by Freeman (1966a), or the ratio of the contour lengths, used by Braunstein (1962). Another contour variable affecting slant judgments in displays of trapezoidal shapes is the relative height of the vertical sides (Figure 5.6). Dunn and Thomas (1966) found an increase in judged slant with increased height of the shorter vertical side.

TEXTURE GRADIENTS VERSUS CONTOUR CONVERGENCE

The relative effectiveness of texture gradients and contour convergence gradients was studied by Clark, Smith, and Rabe (1956a), using four displays of slanted rectangles against unslanted backgrounds: (a) an outline rectangle against homogeneous field; (b) an outline rectangle against textured field containing horizontal lines; (c) a textured rectangle against homogeneous field; and (d) a textured rectangle against textured, lined field (Figure 5.7). All of the displayed slants were 40°, with the right side of the form slanted away from the subject. Judged slant was greatest for the slanted rectangles displayed against homogeneous backgrounds, averaging 15.4° and 13.8° for the textured and untextured rectangles. The difference was not significant. Judged slant was reduced with the textured background, probably because the slanted form was not seen as separate from the background and therefore seemed to be an outline drawn on a flat surface. The overall implications of these results are that contour convergence is more effective in eliciting slant judgments than is a texture density

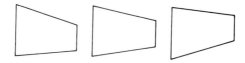

FIGURE 5.6. Variations in the relative heights of vertical sides of figures representing slanted rectangles.

gradient, and that the two factors in combination are no more effective than is contour convergence in isolation. Further support for these implications has been provided by Smith (1964), who found that the addition of texture gradients to trapezoids and slanted rectangles had little effect on judged slant, even when the texture gradient was made to display a direction of slant opposite to that indicated by the contour convergence gradient.

These findings of greater effectiveness of contour convergence than of texture gradients in determining judged slant did not settle the issue of which source of information is actually used by observers in making slant judgments. The issue was further debated by Flock (1965) and Freeman (1965, 1966b). Flock (1964a) had shown geometrically that surface slant could be judged from a texture gradient. He argued that a contour gradient is a special case of a texture gradient. Freeman, pointing to the evidence of the greater effectiveness of contour convergence, argued that a texture gradient is a special case of linear perspective. Both writers were essentially correct. The same perspective information is potentially available from both texture gradients and contour convergence. (This was demonstrated in Chapter 3; see Figure 3.13.) The ease with which human observers extract and process this information may not be the same, however. The use of a texture gradient as an indicator of slant requires the counting of texture elements, or at least some process that matches equal numbers of elements. When converging contours are present, the relative separations of the contours provide the same perspective information, but without the need for a counting or estimation process.

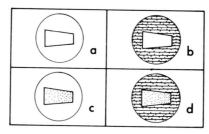

FIGURE 5.7. Combinations of form and background textures. [After Clark, Smith, & Rabe, 1956a.]

Perspective information does not, by itself, provide a veridical indication of surface slant, whether it is derived from a texture gradient or from contour convergence. The size of a surface relative to its distance from the observer determines the relationship between perspective and slant. Flock's theory of the derivation of judged slant from texture gradients takes the relative size and viewing distance into account; Freeman's does not. As a result, Flock predicts veridical slant judgments in all cases while Freeman would expect judged slant to vary with the size and distance of the surface, as well as with its objective slant. The latter view is supported by the findings of Stavrianos (1945) and Freeman (1966a) that the size of slanted rectangles affects judged slant. The situation is complicated, however, by the availability of an additional potential source of slant information in regular forms and textures: form ratio. Though the evidence to be presented in the next section indicates that perspective is more effective than form ratio in determining judged slant in static displays, perspective is not, as we shall see later, the dominant variable in dynamic displays.

FORM RATIO VERSUS PERSPECTIVE

When a surface is rotated about a horizontal or vertical axis, the angle of rotation can be derived from relative changes in the horizontal and vertical positions of projected points on the surface (see Chapter 3). This provides a potential source of slant information, form ratio, that is geometrically independent of perspective. For a surface rotated about a horizontal axis, form ratio is defined as

$$\frac{\dfrac{v}{h}}{\dfrac{V}{H}}$$

where V and H are vertical and horizontal distances on the original surface, and v and h are the projections of these distances when the surface is slanted. The vertical distance in the expression is measured from the axis of rotation, along a line perpendicular to that axis, to a horizontal contour. The horizontal distance is measured along that contour (Figure 5.8). When no horizontal contours are present, form ratio can be measured using other identifiable surface features. Form ratio cannot be determined in a static view of a random texture, however, because there is no way to match the original dimensions to the projected dimensions in the absence of identifiable surface features. When the form ratio can be determined from the projection of a slanted surface, it is equal to the cosine of the slant angle, regardless of viewing distance.

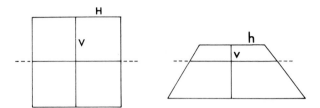

FIGURE 5.8.   Form ratio for a 60° slant.

If, from the form ratio, an observer is to accurately judge slant in a static view of a rotated surface, he must somehow compare the relative projections of horizontal and vertical distances in that view to those in the unslanted surface. This requires an assumption about the original spacing of the contours or of other surface features. If the contours were equally spaced in the unslanted surface, for example, and this assumption of equal spacing were used in the slant judgment process, the resulting judgments would be accurate. The requirement that something be assumed about the original surface is also present in explanations of how perspective factors might lead to veridical slant judgments. The use of contour convergence, for example, assumes that the unslanted surface has parallel contours. The use of a texture gradient to judge slant assumes a uniform distribution of texture elements on the surface. These assumptions, of course, need not be explicitly made by the observer. They can be built into perceptual processes that are automatically applied when the observer attempts to judge surface slant.

Perspective and form ratio can be placed into conflict by artificially producing representations of slanted grid patterns for which perspective at a given viewing distance indicates one slant while the form ratio indicates another. (The patterns produced in this manner are not geometrically possible as projections of slanted surfaces containing equally spaced horizontal and vertical contours.) Braunstein and Payne (1969) produced a series of grid patterns of this type. A dot pattern was also produced corresponding to each grid pattern, displaying a dot at the position of each line intersection in the grid pattern. Examples of these displays are shown in Figure 5.9. The displays were presented in pairs to subjects, who were asked to indicate which member of each pair displayed the greater slant. One group of subjects saw grid patterns only; a second group saw dot patterns only. The results were the same for both groups. When perspective and form ratio were in conflict, 90% of the relative slant judgments were made in accordance with the indications of perspective. There was a slight effect of form ratio on the judgments. The tendency to choose the display with greater slant indicated by perspective increased when the form ratio·rein-

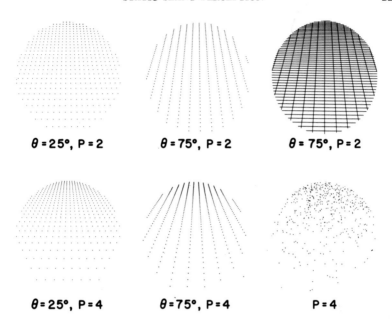

$\theta = 25°$, P = 2 $\theta = 75°$, P = 2 $\theta = 75°$, P = 2

$\theta = 25°$, P = 4 $\theta = 75°$, P = 4   P = 4

FIGURE 5.9. Examples of grid and dot patterns. θ is the $\cos^{-1}$ of the form ratio; P is the perspective ratio. [From Braunstein & Payne, 1969.]

forced rather than conflicted with perspective information. When perspective was constant for both displays in a pair, the display for which the form ratio indicated greater slant was judged to be more slanted with higher-than-chance probability. Similar results were found in a later (unpublished) study in which absolute slant judgments were elicited for individual displays. Judged slant was ordered primarily by perspective, although there was a definite secondary ordering by form ratio, within levels of perspective (Table 5.1). Both variables, then, play a role in the judgment of slant for surfaces of regular textures, but the role of perspective information is clearly dominant. Judged slant was considerably lower for random textures produced at each perspective level (13°, 19°, and 23° for perspective ratios of 2.0, 3.0, and 4.0 respectively; form ratio is not applicable to random textures). It is important to note that these results apply only to static views of slanted surfaces. The findings for transforming displays, as we shall see shortly, are quite different.

BINOCULAR DISPARITY

Binocular disparity can, in isolation, mediate the perception of surface slant. When the same scene is presented to each eye, but the image presented to one eye is expanded horizontally (aniseikonic distortion), the

TABLE 5.1

MEAN SLANT JUDGMENTS IN DEGREES FOR STATIONARY
REGULAR DOT PATTERNS

		Perspective Ratio		
		2.	3.	4.
	25°	22	33	41
Cos⁻¹				
Form	50°	24	35	38
Ratio				
	75°	29	39	42

scene appears to be slanted about a vertical axis (Ogle, 1950). A random dot stereogram based on aniseikonic distortion was shown in Figure 1.27. Gillam (1968) studied the effectiveness of perspective information in reducing the apparent slant produced by aniseikonic distortion. The patterns studied were a random dot pattern, evenly spaced horizontal lines, evenly spaced vertical lines, and a grid. In an initial experiment, the latter two patterns were found to yield more accurate monocular slant judgments than the first two patterns, when displayed rotated about a vertical axis. These patterns were displayed unrotated in a second experiment and observed under aniseikonic distortion. Under those conditions, perspective information indicated flatness and stereopsis indicated rotation about a vertical axis. Slant judgments were greatest under aniseikonic distortion with the two patterns that had produced the smallest slant judgments in the monocular experiment. This indicated that the patterns that were least effective in conveying slant when actually slanted were also least effective in conveying flatness when viewed unslanted under aniseikonic distortion. In general, there appeared to be a compromise between the use of perspective and stereoscopic information in judging slant. This result is similar to that of other investigators who have placed texture gradients and contour convergence in conflict with stereoscopic indicators of slant (Clark, Smith, & Rabe, 1956b; Beck, 1960).

CONCLUSIONS: STATIC DISPLAYS

The research described in the preceding sections provides a reasonably complete picture of the stimulus variables affecting slant perception in static displays: (1) Judged slant is greater for regular than for irregular textures. (2) Regularity in the size and shape of texture elements is more important than regularity in the distribution of the elements. (3) There is an optimum texture density range, below which the texture elements may appear to be independent figures and above which they become fused. (4) Contour convergence is usually more effective in determining judged slant than is a texture gradient. (5) The addition of a texture gradient to a figure with visible contours has little effect on judged slant. (6) Perspective is more effective than form ratio in determining judged slant. (7) When stereoscopic and perspective indications of surface slant are in conflict, judged slant is a compromise between the slants indicated by these two sources.

As clear-cut as these results may seem, there is a serious difficulty limiting their interpretation. The empirical research on slant perception does not provide a means of determining whether increased information about the slant of a surface increases the accuracy of slant judgments or always increases the amount of slant that is judged, regardless of whether this increase leads to a more accurate judgment. This is because judged slant is virtually always an underestimate of displayed slant, due to the presence of conflicting flatness information in most experimental situations. Under these circumstances, an increase in judged slant is always an increase in the accuracy of the slant judgment, making these two variables inseparable.

The problem of separating increased accuracy from increased apparent slant is not well defined for experiments in which surface slant is simulated through the use of photographs of slanted surfaces, shadows, or computer-generated projections. This is especially true when conflicting slant information is deliberately presented. When form ratio and perspective, for example, indicate different slants in a computer-generated projection, is it the slant indicated by perspective or the one indicated by form ratio that is the correct one? Or would the lack of slant indicated by any remaining flatness information in the projection screen be the correct judgment? Accuracy is a meaningful criterion when a slanted surface is directly observed. Under these circumstances we can, and should, ask which variables increase the accuracy with which the slant of a surface is judged and which variables, if any, always tend to make a surface appear more slanted, even when an increase in judged slant results in a less accurate judgment.

One possible way to separate increased accuracy from increased apparent slant would be to find an experimental manipulation that changes accurate slant judgments to overestimates.[2] Consider, for example, a situa-

---

[2] We are concerned here with manipulations that provide increased information about the actual slant of a surface, rather than with "false" slant information. Clark, Smith, and Rabe (1955) showed that cutting a surface in the shape of a trapezoid can increase the judged slant to well above the actual slant.

tion in which a slanted surface containing a random distribution of texture elements is directly observed by subjects, and these subjects accurately judge the slant of the surface. Suppose that a grid pattern were superimposed on the surface and subjects now judged the surface to be more slanted than it actually was. This hypothetical result would indicate that the effect of the grid pattern was to make the surface appear more slanted, rather than to make the slant judgments more accurate. Results of this kind, which would allow a distinction between stimulus variables that increase accuracy and those that always increase apparent slant, are not presently available.

Dynamic Slant Perception

There are several transformations that might be expected to affect the accuracy of slant judgments. The observer might view the actual process of slanting a surface; i.e., the rotation of a surface, usually about the X or Y axis, from the frontal plane to the slant angle that is to be estimated (Figure 5.10a). Other transformations that might be observed would begin with a surface already slanted. A slanted surface might be translated along the axis of slant (usually the X or Y axis). A surface slanted with the top away from the observer, for example, might be moved horizontally across the observer's field of view (Figure 5.10b). A slanted surface might be translated along the Z axis, moving toward or away from the observer while maintaining a constant slant (Figure 5.10c). Studies in which the observer views the rotation of a surface from a frontal position to a slant, and studies in which translations of a slanted surface along the axis of slant are observed will be described next. The translation of slanted surfaces along the Z axis does not appear to have been

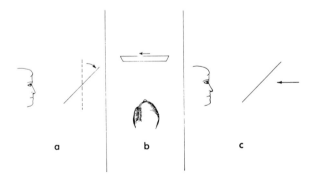

a   b   c

FIGURE 5.10.   Stimulus situations for the study of dynamic slant perception.

investigated, but the evidence cited in Chapter IV on the perception of relative depth in patterns undergoing this transformation suggests that it would lead to accurate slant judgments. Rotation about the Z axis, because of its ambiguity, is probably not of interest in the study of dynamic slant perception.

ROTATION TO A SLANT

The effect of actually observing the rotation process on the accuracy of slant judgments was studied by Gibson and Gibson (1957) using polar projections of four patterns: "An amoeboid group of amoeboid dark shapes or spots (the irregular texture), a solid amoeboid contour form (the irregular form), a square group of dark squares (the regular texture), and a solid square (the regular form) [p. 132]." The patterns were rotated to angles of 15°, 30°, 45°, 60°, or 70°. Each trial consisted of 10 cycles of oscillation between the frontal position and one of the five angles of rotation. Subjects responded by adjusting a circular model to the angle of maximum apparent slant. Slant judgments were highly accurate for all patterns when the transformation sequence was observed. There was little difference among the patterns in accuracy of slant judgments, although these judgments were slightly more accurate for the regular patterns.

The results were quite different for a control group that saw each pattern motionless at a 60° slant. The irregular patterns were judged to be in the plane of the screen on 85% of the trials. The regular stimuli appeared unslanted on 3% of the trials. The mean judged slant for the regular stimuli was 24°, as compared to 61° in the group that observed the patterns in motion. These results dramatically demonstrated the effect of observing the transformation sequence on judgments of surface slant. The dynamic viewing condition yielded accurate slant judgments, compared to judgments of less than half the actual slant in the static condition. Texture regularity, a critical variable in static slant judgments, had little effect when the patterns were observed in motion.

Form Ratio and Perspective. What information in the transformation sequence does the subject actually use in making slant judgments? Two potential sources of slant information in dynamic displays, as in static displays, are form ratio and perspective. Just as the slants indicated by these two sources can be varied independently in static displays, these factors can be separated when the transformation sequence is displayed. The display of the transformation sequence might be expected to strengthen the role of form ratio in determining judged slant. The use of form ratio requires the comparison of a slanted form to an assumed original form. Even instructing subjects with a model showing equal spacing between texture elements in both the horizontal and vertical dimensions (Braunstein & Payne, 1969) does not necessarily lead to the incorporation of this assumption in the perceptual processes underlying slant judgments. Actually displaying the transformation from the original form to the slanted form, on the other hand, should have this effect. The increased role of form ratio in slant judgments when the transformation sequence is observed was demonstrated in an unpublished study by Braunstein and Payne. Motion picture sequences were generated in which one of three slants was indicated by form ratio and one of three slants was indicated by perspective. These nine combinations of form ratio and perspective were displayed with either regular or random dot patterns. Each sequence displayed a plane starting in a frontal position, moving to the specified combination of form ratio and perspective, returning to the frontal position, and finally returning to the slanted position. Subjects used a model to indicate judged slant. The results for regular dot patterns are shown in Table 5.2. Form ratio was clearly the dominant factor. Judged slant was ordered primarily by form ratio and ordered by perspective within levels of form ratio. These results can be contrasted with those obtained in the study using stationary displays, discussed earlier (Table 5.1). In that study, judged slant was ordered primarily by perspective and ordered by form ratio within levels of perspective.

The results with random textures were similar to those of Gibson and Gibson (1957). When the transformation was displayed, texture regularity had little effect on judged slant. This can be compared to the results with stationary displays of random textures varying in perspective, which elicited considerably lower slant judgments than stationary displays of regular patterns.

These results suggest that the importance of viewing the transformation

TABLE 5.2

MEAN SLANT JUDGMENTS IN DEGREES FOR REGULAR DOT PATTERNS IN MOTION

		Perspective Ratio		
		2.	3.	4.
Cos^{-1} Form Ratio	25°	28	33	37
	50°	39	44	46
	75°	54	58	58

sequence may result from the need to actually observe the relative horizontal and vertical changes before form ratio can be used effectively. Form ratio indicates degree of slant but not direction of slant. Direction information would have to come from perspective indications. The perception of degree of slant is closely related to the perception of rotary motion. The difference is that rotary motion is usually studied with one or more 360° cycles, while slant is studied with rotations to angles of less than 90° from the frontal plane. Like the perception of degree of slant, the perception of rotary motion does not depend on perspective changes. Rotary motion in depth is as likely to be reported with parallel projections, lacking in perspective changes, as with polar projections (see Chapter 4). Direction of rotation, on the other hand, can be correctly determined only in polar projections (see Chapter 6). This is likely to hold for direction of slant as well, although partial rotations have not been studied with parallel projections. The perception of degree of slant and that of direction of slant appear to be based on separate processes using separate, and potentially independent, sources of information. These are likely to be the same processes underlying depth and direction judgments, respectively, in the more general case of the perception of rotation in depth.

TRANSLATION OF SLANTED SURFACES

Translating a slanted surface along the axis of slant sets up a velocity gradient in the retinal projection: The velocities of the projected elements vary inversely with their distance from the observer. This is purely a perspective effect. In a parallel projection of a translating slanted surface, the projected velocities of all texture elements are identical. The translation of a slanted surface is a general case of motion parallax. There is no dynamic form ratio information available because the change from the unslanted to the slanted surface is not seen. Comparisons of the accuracy of slant judgments for stationary and slanted surfaces therefore provide a straightforward measure of the effectiveness of a velocity gradient as a carrier of perspective information.

Flock (1962, 1964b) obtained slant judgments for shadow projections of stationary and translating textured surfaces. The surfaces had been rotated about the X axis, with either the top or bottom slanted away from the observer. The slanted surfaces were either stationary or were displayed translating along the X axis. They were observed monocularly through an aperture that concealed the borders of the surface. Flock varied the rate of motion (.07, .12, and .26 ft per sec) and the regularity of the texture (irregular patterns or grid patterns). Slant judgments were highly accurate for all of the motion conditions and the rate of motion and texture regularity had little effect. Judged slant, across a variety of motion rates and textures, averaged 2°, 8°, 18°, 27°, and 38° for physical slants of 0°, 10°, 20°, 30°, and 40°. The results for static slants were similar to those of studies previously described. Slants were generally underestimated, though accuracy was greater for the regular textures. Judged slant was 2°, 5°, 12°, 21°, and 31° for the regular textures and 8°, 7°, 8°, 10°, and 15° for the irregular textures for the five physical slants listed above. (The data in this section are from Conditions 1–11, Flock, 1962). Motion clearly had increased the accuracy of slant judgments, especially for the irregular textures.

Further evidence for the dominant role of velocity gradients in determining judged slant for surfaces translating along the axis of slant was provided by Braunstein (1968). Braunstein used a computer animation technique to produce motion picture sequences in which the velocity gradient could represent one slant angle and the texture gradient another. This was accomplished by starting with a random uniform texture and making two independent computations for each texture element in each sequence: (*a*) the initial location of each texture element, based on the slant angle selected for the texture gradient, and (*b*) the amount of horizontal displacement of the element from frame to frame, based on the slant angle selected for the velocity gradient. Sixteen sequences displayed combinations of texture gradients representing slants of 0°, 20°, 40, and 60° with velocity gradients representing the same four angles of rotation. Four additional sequences displayed stationary texture gradients corresponding to the four slant angles. Figure 5.11 shows the effects of these combinations of velocity and texture gradients on judged slant. Slant judgments were affected by both gradients, but the weight (computed by linear regression) given velocity information was more than twice that given texture information.

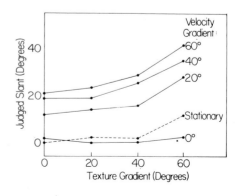

FIGURE 5.11. Effects of combinations of texture and velocity gradients on judged slant.

Conclusion

The research on static slant judgments discussed in the first section of this chapter is useful in suggesting variables to be investigated in dynamic slant perception, but it is clear that the results obtained in the static case do not generalize directly to the dynamic case. Even for the few variables that have been studied in both static and dynamic displays, striking differences have been found. The dominance of perspective over form ratio in determining slant judgments is reversed when rotation to a slant is displayed. The increase in judged slant with increased texture regularity is absent when either rotation to a slant or translation of a slanted surface along the axis of slant is displayed. Judged slant was close to displayed slant in most studies involving either of these transformations, in contrast to the underestimates of 50% or more found with static displays. These results, reinforced by the results obtained when motion and texture gradients are placed in conflict, suggest that motion overrides static indicators of slant, completely dominating slant judgments. All of the variables that have proved of importance in static slant judgments have not as yet been studied in transforming displays, however. Most notably, the effects of disparity on slant judgments have not been compared to the effects of motion. When disparity and motion are separately compared to static perspective information, disparity does not seem to be as clearly dominant as motion, but this is only an indirect answer to the question of how conflicting motion and disparity information will affect perceived slant.

6

Perceived Direction of Rotary Motion

WHEN AN OBJECT IS ROTATED about a vertical (Y) or horizontal (X) axis, there are continuous changes in the depth relationships of parts of that object. Parts that were at one time closer to the observer move further away, and parts that were further away move closer. There is a complete reversal of depth relationships with each 180° of rotation. The accuracy with which observers can respond to these changing relationships can tell us a great deal about the process underlying depth perception in dynamic displays. It is not surprising that there has been a considerable amount of research on factors influencing the accuracy of judgments of direction of rotary motion. This research has proceeded along two separate lines, which have only recently become fully merged: research with shadows and computer simulations of rotating objects, and research involving direct observation of rotating objects. The following sections will consider the principal findings of these two lines of research, and their eventual combination in several recent studies. The

131

results of these studies will form the basis for a model of the perception of rotary motion, to be discussed in the remaining sections of the chapter.

Shadow and Computer Projections

The ambiguity of direction of rotation judgments under certain conditions was the essential feature of two related illusions described in Chapter 2, the windmill illusion and the fan illusion. Direction of rotation judgments were also included in most of the studies described in Chapter 4 that dealt with rotation about the X or Y axes. Those studies were concerned mainly with identifying the conditions under which the transformation studied elicited reports of motion in depth. A major objective of that research was the isolation of the effects of motion by eliminating disparity, convergence, and accommodation as potential indicators of the relative distances of parts of the rotating object. This was accomplished in the earlier studies by displaying shadows of rotating objects, of three-dimensional wire figures (Wallach & O'Connell, 1953), and of slides containing regular and irregular textures and forms (Gibson & Gibson, 1957). Later studies used computer animation techniques to display random line and dot patterns (Braunstein, 1962, 1966; Green, 1961) and transforming solid angles of light (Johansson, 1964).

Some of the studies using shadow projection techniques found an ambiguity in the perceived direction of rotation comparable to that found in the windmill and fan illusions (e.g., by Wallach and O'Connell, 1953), but others (e.g., Gibson and Gibson, 1957) found no such ambiguity. In the original observations of the windmill and fan illusions, the viewing distances were sufficiently great as to approximate parallel projections of the rotating objects. These projections carry no information about direction of rotation (see Chaper 3). In the Wallach and O'Connell experiments, a shadow projection system was used in which the light source was relatively distant from the rotating object. This arrangement approximated a parallel projection. Gibson and Gibson, on the other hand, used a polar projection in their shadow transformer. The projection lamp was relatively close to the transforming object.

Braunstein (1966) directly compared accuracy of direction judgments with parallel and polar projections, using computer-animated displays of random dot patterns representing two-dimensional or three-dimensional configurations of points rotating about the X or Y axis. Direction of rotation judgments for the parallel projections were a chance matter (51% correct). Accuracy was high for polar projections, however, averaging 90% correct. These results provided direct support for the finding of the earlier studies with rotating silhouettes: Accuracy of direction judgments is determined by the distance of the projection point in the display system, ranging from high accuracy with a close projection point (polar projection) to chance performance with an infinitely distant projection point (parallel projection).[1]

Direct Observation of Rotating Figures

The studies reviewed in the preceeding section can be thought of as a continuing line of research, initially inspired by the discovery of the windmill illusion, proceeding with specially developed shadow displays, and most recently using computer animation techniques to isolate sources of information affecting depth perception in rotating objects. This line of research did not include the study of another illusion described in Chapter 2, the rotating trapezoid illusion. This illusion, which was discovered much later than the windmill illusion, gave rise to an independent line of research. This seems to have occurred largely because the original demonstrations of the trapezoid illusion were conducted under conditions of direct vision rather than with silhouettes of rotating objects.

Ames' (1951) initial finding was that a rotating trapezoid appeared to oscillate under certain viewing conditions, although the motion of a rotating rectangle was correctly perceived under the same conditions. A number of rectangular and trapezoidal forms were examined by Ames in preliminary studies. These are shown in Figure 6.1. The trapezoidal plane surface in Row (a) was least effective in producing the illusion. The frame-shaped trapezoidal surface in Row (b) was more effective; the surface in Row (c) was even more so. The effectiveness of the illusion was increased by the addition of shadows in Row (d), a finding which has been confirmed by Cross and Cross (1969) for other objects as well as trapezoids. Adding "panes" in Rows (e) and (f) and increasing the degree of trapezoidal variation (the difference in the length of the vertical sides) also increased the effectiveness of the illusion.

Ames considered the rotating trapezoid illusion to be a major demonstration of the validity of his "transactional" theory of perception. According to this theory, perception consists of "an implicit awareness of the probable significance for action" of the present pattern of sensory input

---

[1] In direct vision, the projection point is the nodal point of the eye. When a shadow projection technique is used, the projection point is a function of the position of the light source. The projection point is a theoretical entity in a computer program when computer animation is used.

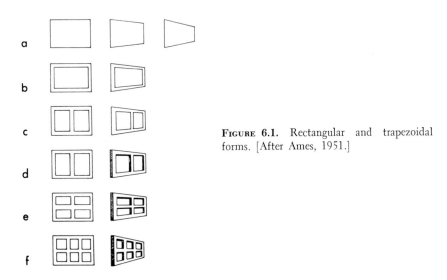

FIGURE 6.1. Rectangular and trapezoidal forms. [After Ames, 1951.]

based on assumptions derived from past experience with similar inputs (Kilpatrick, 1952, p. 89). The transactional explanation of the rotating trapezoid illusion was as follows: The observer has had considerable prior experience requiring action to be taken with respect to rectangular forms, such as going through doors and locating windows. He has learned to interpret particular degrees of trapezoidal retinal projections of these rectangular forms in terms of the positioning of the form relative to his line of sight. He consequently unconsciously assumes the trapezoidal projections that occur during rotation of the trapezoidal window to be the projections of a rectangular window at varying slants. As a result of this assumption, he judges the side having the longer retinal projection to be the closer side throughout the rotation cycle. But when the object is a trapezoid, the longer retinal projection may be produced by the more distant side. This will occur during the half of the rotation cycle when the more distant side is also the objectively longer side (Figure 6.2), and results in a misperception of the relative distance of the two sides during that half of the cycle. Misperceived direction of rotary motion then occurs in the following manner, according to the transactional explanation: Rotation of a form, following its presentation in a frontal position, is perceived when the total horizontal projection of the form decreases. If the left side of the form appears farther away, for example, during this overall horizontal decrease, past experience with rectangular forms dictates that clockwise rotation will be perceived. The apparent slant of the form thus determines its apparent direction of rotation. A rotating trapezoid is perceived as oscillating because its orientation is misperceived

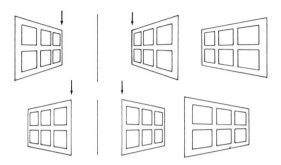

FIGURE 6.2. Projections of a rotating trapezoid at 45° intervals. The arrows indicate the more distant edge in the 45°, 135°, 225° and 315° views. The top row shows the veridical portion of the rotation sequence; the bottom row shows the nonveridical portion. The simulated viewing distance is 6 times the width of the trapezoid.

during about half of the rotation cycle, and its direction of rotation is therefore perceptually reversed during that portion of the cycle.

There is a serious flaw in this explanation of the apparent oscillation of a rotating trapezoid. The rotating trapezoid appears to change in size and shape during rotation, as well as in apparent direction. Ames reported these observations and presented a reasonable explanation in terms of the projective geometry of the situation The projections of the longer side are greater when that side is physically closer than when it is physically more distant but appears closer. Similarly, the projections of the shorter side are not as great when it is physically more distant as when it is closer but appears more distant. The retinal projections of the rotating trapezoid are systematically different for the veridical and nonveridical portions of the rotation sequence (see Figure 6.2). They could not represent projections of a constant rectangle, and if they are perceived as representing an oscillating rectangle, it would have to be of a rectangle that changed its size and shape while oscillating. This is where the Ames explanation falters. It resorts to geometry at this point and neglects the principal basis for the transactional explanation, past experience. The acceptance of apparent size and shape change of an assumed rectangle implies that the observer has had more experience with rectangular windows that change their physical shape and size when they are observed from different angles than with windows that are trapezoidal in shape. Put another way, the Ames explanation implies that past experience produces a stronger tendency to perceive objects as rectangular than to perceive objects as rigid.

Most other explanations also attribute misperceived direction of rotary motion of a trapezoid to misperceived initial slant. They differ from the

Ames explanation in the manner in which they account for the misperception of the slant of the trapezoid. Pastore (1952) disputed Ames' empiricist explanation, pointing out that past experience with rectangular windows could not account for the findings of apparent oscillation which he had obtained with a variety of shapes in addition to the trapezoid. These shapes included a circle, ellipses, a triangle, a diamond, a hemispherical arc, a V-shaped cutout, and even a rectangle. Pastore suggests that the tendency to perceive a trapezoid as a slanted rectangle may be due to central processes of the type advanced by Gestalt psychologists. An example of such a process, which would be relevant to the trapezoid illusion, would be a tendency to perceive increased symmetry in asymmetrical shapes.

Graham (1963) suggested it was linear perspective that caused the longer side of the trapezoid to appear closer. He also concluded that there was no veridical direction information even potentially available in the retinal projection of a rotating trapezoid. Graham's analysis was appropriate to parallel projections only, for polar projections do contain such information. His analysis was therefore inappropriate for direct vision, in which only polar projections occur (Hershberger, 1967).

Power and Day (1973) proposed that the apparent direction of rotary motion for plane objects is based on the apparent orientation of the objects. Their theory was not unlike earlier explanations of misperceived rotary motion based on misperceived initial slant. The major difference was in their generalization of the basis of misperceived orientation from misleading linear perspective in the overall shape of the object to misleading linear perspective in patterns superimposed on the object. The plane objects studied were ellipses that were either unpatterned or had line patterns painted on their surface. The patterns consisted either of horizontal lines or of lines converging toward a vanishing point to the right or left of the ellipse. The frequencies of apparent reversal were lowest for the ellipses with horizontal lines, highest for the ellipses with converging lines (with direction of rotation misperceived when the edge nearest the vanishing point was closest to the observer), and intermediate for the unpatterned ellipses. When the orientation of the ellipses was judged before they were observed in motion, judgments were accurate with the horizontal pattern, systematically inaccurate with the converging line pattern (with the edge nearest the vanishing point tending to appear slanted away from the observer), and considerably variable for the unpatterned ellipse. Power and Day used these findings to support their hypothesis that "apparent direction of movement is determined by apparent direction of orientation [p. 220]" when stimuli for orientation are available. They did not, however, provide direct evidence for this hypothesis, either in their experiment with plane objects or in a second experiment with three-dimensional objects. They showed that converging contour lines, even if painted on an object that does not itself have linear contours, result in misperceived orientation and that converging contour lines result in misperceived direction of rotary motion, but not that misperception of orientation determines misperception of rotary motion. The evidence presented in Chapter 5 of the dominant role of dynamic factors in slant perception would suggest that static orientation information is not likely to determine judgments in a dynamic situation. It is more probable that dynamic changes in the projections of the converging line patterns determine the perceived direction of rotary motion.

Combining the Two Lines of Research

The two lines of research summarized in the preceding sections led to two general conclusions: (1) Accuracy in judging direction of rotation decreases with increased viewing distance. (2) Accuracy is greater for some forms (e.g., rectangles) than for others (e.g., trapezoids). These conclusions can be generalized into the following hypothesis concerning the perception of rotary motion: With a sufficiently distant projection point, the direction of rotation of any form may be misperceived, and certain forms give rise to systematic misperceptions. With closer projection points, the direction of rotation of some forms will be correctly perceived though that of other forms will still be misperceived. With a close enough projection point, the direction of rotation of any form will be correctly perceived. This hypothesis was tested by Braunstein and Payne (1968a), using computer-generated motion picture sequences representing rectangles, trapezoids, circles, and ellipses rotating about a vertical axis. Each sequence showed one 360° rotation at 8 rpm. There were five projection points used in the computation of these displays. One projection point was located at infinity, yielding a parallel projection. The four others were polar projection points located at distances from the axis of rotation equal to 4.5, 2.5, 1.8, and 1.5 times the width of the rotating figure. ,

Accuracy of direction judgments did not exceed chance levels for forms displayed through parallel projections, but the type of error varied with the form. The direction of rotation of the rectangle was accurately reported for the entire 360° cycle in one-quarter of the observations, and inaccurately reported for the entire cycle in approximately one-quarter of the observations. Reversal of direction during a 360° cycle was reported in the remaining half of the observations. In contrast, oscillation was reported in every 360° cycle when the trapezoid was displayed with a parallel projection. With polar projections, accuracy increased with decreasing projection point distance for all forms, but increased most rapidly for the rectangle. These results confirmed the hypothesis that projection distance and figure shape interact to determine the accuracy of direction judgments.

Other stimulus sequences were included in the experiment for the purpose of obtaining a more precise understanding of the stimulus variables underlying the interaction of projection distance and shape. These special sequences, referred to as "horizontal perspective" sequences and "vertical perspective" sequences, were not physically possible transformations of rigid objects. In a horizontal perspective sequence, the horizontal distances in the projection of the rotating form were determined by the geometry of polar projection, while vertical distances were computed using the geometry of parallel projection. The reverse was true for vertical perspective sequences. Vertical distances in the projections were based on polar projections and horizontal distances were computed using a parallel projection. Figure 6.3 shows a rectangle in the frontal position and slanted rectangles displayed through an ordinary polar projection, a horizontal perspective projection and a vertical perspective projection.[2]

Accuracy of direction judgments for rotating rectangles and trapezoids increased about as rapidly with decreasing projection point distance, when this distance affected only the vertical dimension of the projected image, as when it affected both dimensions. When distance changes affected the horizontal dimension only, accuracy exceeded chance levels at all polar projection distances, but remained well below the levels reached with normal and vertical perspective. It was concluded that the changes in the image projected by a rotating rectangle or trapezoid that most affect accuracy of direction of rotation judgments are in the dimension parallel to the axis of rotation, which was vertical in that study. Changes in the other dimension appeared to have a secondary effect. This implies that direction judgments are affected by at least one primary factor related to changes in the dimension parallel to the axis of rotation, and by at least one secondary factor related to changes in the perpendicular dimension of the projected image.

---

[2] It is important to note that the preceding description of horizontal and vertical perspective variations assumes a vertical axis of rotation. To be as general as possible, the expressions "perspective changes in the dimension perpendicular to the axis of rotation" and "perspective changes in the dimension parallel to the axis of rotation" should be substituted for "horizontal perspective" and "vertical perspective," respectively. The shorter expressions will be used here, with the understanding that their meaning would be reversed if the forms were rotating about a horizontal axis.

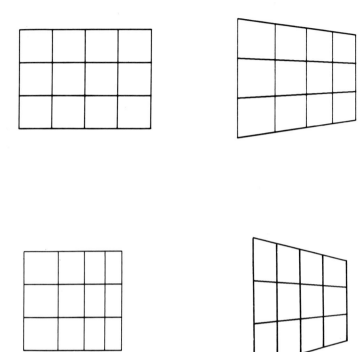

Figure 6.3. Projections of a rectangle (upper left) rotated about a vertical axis, displayed with a polar projection (upper right), with horizontal changes affected only by a polar projection (lower left), and with vertical changes affected only by a polar projection (lower right). [From Braunstein, 1972.]

The greater effectiveness of vertical perspective changes relative to horizontal perspective changes was confirmed by Jansson and Börjesson (1969) using oscilloscope-generated displays of horizontally moving points and lines. Accuracy was near chance for displays simulating polar projections of a single rotating point, which would show horizontal perspective effects only. Accuracy of direction judgments exceeded 90% for displays of a single vertical line that changed in length as it moved horizontally, simulating the vertical perspective changes that occur during polar projections of rotary motion.

Changes in the horizontal dimension alone can mediate better-than-chance judgments of direction of rotation if more than one point is shown in rotation. Judgments based on horizontal changes apparently require the observation of relative motions in that dimension. Hershberger and his associates (Hershberger & Urban, 1970a, b; Hershberger & Carpenter, 1972; Hershberger, Carpenter, Starzec, & Laughlin, 1974; Hershberger & Starzec,

1974) obtained better-than-chance judgments of direction of rotary motion for computer-generated displays simulating polar projections of a rigid dotted horizontal line rotating about a vertical axis. The positions of the dots in these displays changed in the horizontal dimension only. By manipulating the ratio of the accelerations of the dots to their distances from the axis of rotation, with other indications of direction of rotation controlled, Hershberger, Carpenter, Starzec, and Laughlin (1974) obtained veridical judgments of direction of rotation when the acceleration/displacement gradient accurately simulated the gradient in a polar projection (the gradient normally increases as the dots approach). They obtained nonveridical judgments when the gradient was made opposite to that found in polar projections. Judgments were equivocal when the acceleration/displacement ratio of each dot was the same, simulating a parallel projection.

In order to further specify the sources of information used in direction of rotation judgments, Braunstein (1971) developed a series of forms that combined geometrical features of rectangles and trapezoids. These features were encompassed in three factors: (1) the angles between the horizontal and vertical contours; (2) the extents of the vertical contours; and (3) the position of the axis of rotation relative to the vertical contours. The first two of these variables are illustrated in Figure 6.4. The rows show the six angle combinations, and the columns show the three side variations. The axis of rotation was either at the horizontal center of the form (symmetric) or displaced to the right (asymmetric). (In the Ames trapezoid and in those studied by Braunstein and Payne, 1968a, the axis of rotation was closer to the shorter vertical side.) Each form was displayed undergoing one complete rotation about a vertical axis at 8 rpm. Each display was produced with one of five projection points, located at distances from the axis of rotation equal to 40, 20, 10, 5, and 2.5 times the width of the form. Accuracy of direction judgments increased with decreasing projection distance for each form. Accuracy was highest for the forms most like rectangles such as form (a), lowest for those most like trapezoids such as forms (h) and (o), and intermediate for the forms that combined features of rectangles and trapezoids. For the intermediate forms, accuracy was ordered primarily by angle relationships, secondly by side relationships, and affected only slightly by the position of the axis of rotation. Consider, for example, forms (g) and (m), which have unequal vertical contour lengths appropriate to a trapezoid but display right angles appropriate to a rectangle. These forms may be contrasted to forms (b) and (c), which have equal vertical contours, as does a rectangle, but display acute angles on one side and obtuse angles on the other, as in a trapezoid. Accuracy was higher for (g) and (m)

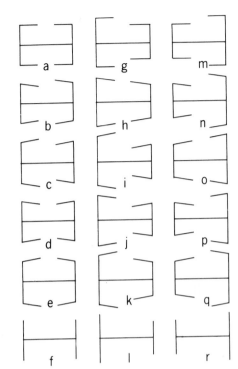

FIGURE 6.4. Forms combining rectangular and trapezoidal features. [From Braunstein, 1971.]

than for (b) and (c). These results, combined with those of Braunstein and Payne (1968a), indicated that changes in the angles between the horizontal and vertical contours in the projections of rotating figures constitute the principal source of information used by subjects in direction of rotation judgments. Similar conclusions were reached by Börjesson

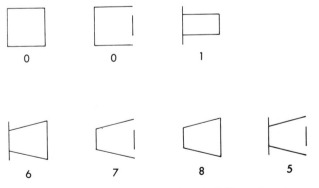

FIGURE 6.5. Forms varying in relative lengths of vertical sides and contour convergence. The number of subjects reporting oscillation for each pattern is indicated ($N = 8$). [After Börjesson, 1971.]

(1971), using other forms in which the relative lengths of the vertical sides were varied independently of the convergence of the horizontal contours. Figure 6.5 shows these forms, and indicates the number of oscillations reported for each. Börjesson concluded that "patterns with straight edges perpendicular to the axis of rotation are correctly perceived to rotate, but patterns with converging edges are perceived to oscillate with the end of the greatest distance between the converging edges closest to the S [p. 305]."

A Model of the Perception of Rotary Motion

An explanation of the perception of direction of rotary motion must take into account the following general findings of the studies presented in the preceding section:

1. The distance of the projection point from the axis of rotation, relative to the width of the form, determines accuracy of rotation judgments for all forms. Accuracy of judgments based on parallel projections cannot exceed chance levels.

2. Accuracy increases most rapidly with decreasing projection distance when the angles between the horizontal and vertical contours are right angles, provided that perspective effects are displayed in the dimension parallel to the axis of rotation ("vertical" perspective if the axis is vertical). It is perspective effects in the dimension parallel to the axis of rotation that cause the projections of the contour angles to vary systematically with direction of rotation.

3. Accuracy increases least rapidly with decreasing projection distance when the angles between the contours are acute on one side of the axis of rotation and obtuse on the other side. The increase in accuracy is greatest with perspective variation in both dimensions and least with variation only in the dimension perpendicular to the axis of rotation ("horizontal" perspective).

These findings can be explained without resorting to an hypothesis about misperception of the shape of trapezoids. Instead, we will assume that the observer processes the same information in the same manner for both rotating rectangles and rotating trapezoids and that this information is dynamic rather than static. First, there must be at least two sources of information. Changes that are based on vertical perspective appear dominant; changes based on horizontal perspective have a secondary effect on direction judgments. In a polar projection of a rotating rectangle, vertical perspective changes cause the angles between the horizontal and vertical contours to decrease as a side approaches and increase as a side recedes. This information could be used to correctly judge direction of rotation. Figure 6.6a and Figure 6.6b show the changes in the projected shape of a rotating rectangle displayed with parallel and polar projections. In the case of a rotating trapezoid, increases and decreases in these angles are affected by the shape of the trapezoid as well as by vertical perspective variations. When the projection of the side enclosed by acute angles approaches the axis of rotation, these angles may decrease regardless of whether the side is approaching or receding. This occurs even in a parallel projection (Figure 6.6c). When the projection point is close enough, however, the effect of vertical perspective can overcome the effect of the trapezoidal shape, and the acute angles will decrease only briefly, if at all, when the side is receding (Figure 6.6d).

Consider a subject judging the approach of a side of a rectangle or trapezoid, using the following processing rule based on these contour angle changes: If the angles between the contours on one side are decreasing, that side is approaching. This rule would result in the following perceptual judgments:

1. For rectangles displayed without vertical perspective variations, judgments would be a chance matter.

2. For rectangles displayed with detectable vertical perspective variations, the subject would correctly judge the direction of rotation.

3. For trapezoids displayed either without vertical perspective variations or with variations too small to overcome the effects of the trapezoidal shape on contour angle changes: (a) direction judgments would be correct when the projection of the side enclosed by acute angles moves towards the axis of rotation if that side is approaching; (b) direction judg-

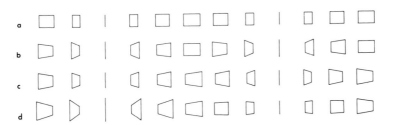

FIGURE 6.6. Changes in the projected shape of rotating figures, at 30° intervals: (a) a rectangle, parallel projection; (b) a rectangle, polar projection; (c) a trapezoid, parallel projection; (d) a trapezoid, polar projection. The simulated viewing distance in the polar projections is 1.67 times the width of the form.

ments would be incorrect when the projection of the side enclosed by acute angles moves towards the axis of rotation if that side is receding. Judgments would, consequently, be of oscillation.

4. With a close enough projection point, the subject would judge the direction of rotation of a trapezoid correctly throughout the transformation sequence.

The use of this rule would not explain the effects of horizontal perspective variations. A secondary source of information must be postulated. In a polar projection of a rotating rectangle, horizontal perspective changes cause the approaching side to accelerate more rapidly than the receding side as the rectangle leaves the frontal plane. This occurs if the vertical sides of the rectangle are equidistant from the axis of rotation. If they are not equidistant (as in the case of the Ames trapezoid which had the shorter side closer to the axis of rotation), the vertical side that is more distant from the axis tends to accelerate more rapidly. This is true even for parallel projections. In the case of polar projections, a sufficiently close projection point can cause the effects of horizontal perspective changes to overcome the effects of unequal distance of the sides from the axis of rotation. This would result in the approaching side accelerating more rapidly during most or all of the rotation cycle.

Consider now a subject judging the approach of a side of a rectangle or trapezoid on the basis of the following rule: When the form leaves the frontal position, the side that is accelerating more rapidly is approaching. (Assume that the sides of the rectangle are equidistant from the axis of rotation but the shorter side of the trapezoid is closer to that axis than is the longer side.) This rule would produce the following direction judgments:

1. For rectangles displayed without horizontal perspective variations, judgments would be a chance matter.

2. For rectangles displayed with detectable horizontal perspective variations, the subject would correctly judge the direction of rotation.

3. For trapezoids displayed either without horizontal perspective variations or with variations too small to overcome the effects of the unequal distances of the vertical sides from the axis of rotation on the relative acceleration of the sides: (a) direction judgments would be correct when the projection of the side farthest from the axis of rotation moves toward that axis if that side is approaching; (b) direction judgments would be incorrect when the projection of the side farthest from the axis moves toward that axis if that side is receding. Judgments would, consequently, be of oscillation.

4. With a close enough projection point, the subject would judge the direction of rotation of a trapezoid correctly throughout the transformation sequence.

The evidence presented earlier suggests that the first rule is dominant. We will assume that the second rule is applied only when there is insufficient information for the application of the first rule (i.e., no detectable contour angle changes). The following model can then be constructed to account for the responses in studies of rotating rectangles and trapezoids:

Before judging direction of rotation the subject must decide

whether he is observing a rigid form, and
whether the form is rotating in three-dimensional space.
These two related judgments are not handled in the present model. The variables underlying the perception of rotary motion in depth are still not adequately understood, but appear to be separable from those that determine accuracy of direction judgments (see Chapter 4).

If the form is judged to be rigid and rotating, its direction is judged in the following manner:

One of the vertical sides is considered. (This choice is arbitrary in the present model.)
A decision is made as to whether that side is approaching or receding:
If changes in the angles between that side and the projection of the horizontal sides are detectable, then
if the angle is increasing, the side is judged to be receding, or
if the angle is decreasing the side is judged to be approaching.
If changes in the angles are not detectable, then if changes in the relative acceleration of the vertical sides are detectable, the side that is accelerating more rapidly is judged to be approaching.
If neither change is detectable, the judgment of which side is approaching is made on some other basis that will tentatively be approximated by a random choice.
If the side is judged to be approaching, then
If it is to the right of the axis of rotation, a clockwise direction is judged.
Otherwise a counterclockwise direction is judged.

If the side is judged to be receding, then

If it is to the right of the axis of rotation a counterclockwise direction is judged.

Otherwise a clockwise direction is judged.

Figure 6.7 presents the model in flow chart form. The Experimenter Routine is not part of the model but it included to show the nature of the stimulus input to the Subject Model. The information provided to the Subject Model is the same as that used to plot frames of computer-generated motion pictures for use in experiments with human subjects (Braunstein, 1962, 1966, 1971; Braunstein & Payne, 1968a).

The first three decisions in the Subject Model are not fully specified in this version of the model. This is because of a lack of sufficient data on the processes involved in these decisions. Instead, the "yes" branch is used in these three tests. This does not present a problem when the model's application is limited to the perception of rotating rectangles and trapezoids. The perception of a rigid form undergoing rotary (including oscillatory) motion occurs almost without exception for these stimuli. The selected side makes little difference. These steps would have to be specified before the model could be applied to a wider range of stimuli.

The central decision in the model, "Is the selected side approaching?," is handled in a subroutine. This question is asked at only two positions during each 360° rotation. This implies that changes in perceived direction of rotation occur within a small interval ($\beta°$) after the form leaves the frontal position (0° or 180°). This result has been obtained in several studies, with a variety of forms (Cook, Mefferd, & Wieland, 1967; Day & Power, 1965; Epstein, Jansson, & Johansson, 1968; Graham & Gillam, 1970). If the rotation sequence is at $\beta°$ or at $180° + \beta°$, the first decision criterion is checked. If the absolute change in the angle between the selected vertical side and an adjacent segment exceeds a subject sensitivity parameter, the decision of whether the side is approaching is made on the basis of that criterion. The second criterion is considered if the first criterion does not exceed the sensitivity parameter. If the difference in acceleration of the two vertical sides does not exceed a second sensitivity parameter, the decision is made by a random process.

Once the decision of whether the selected side is approaching is made by the subroutine, the judgment of direction of rotation by the Subject Model is straightforward. It is assumed that the subject can judge the location of the axis of rotation, which is obvious at 90° and 270°, and can easily determine whether the projection of the selected side is moving to the left or to the right across his field of view.

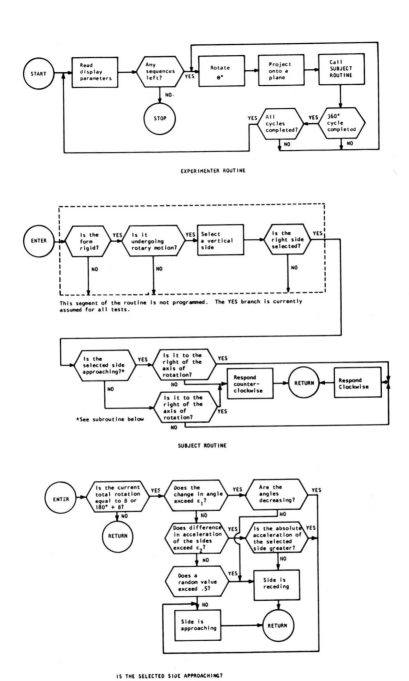

FIGURE 6.7. A model for the perception of rotating figures. [From Braunstein, 1972.]

Evaluation of the Model

The model was tested with a set of subject sensitivity parameters and a position sampling parameter selected to enable it to approximate the quantitative results of Braunstein and Payne (1968a) and unpublished detailed results summarized by Braunstein (1971). The model results were based on 100 simulated subjects. Each subject was assigned to one of three levels of sensitivity to contour angle changes for rectangles and to one of three different levels of sensitivity to contour angle changes for trapezoids. The use of two sets of sensitivity parameters for angle changes reflects the hypothesis (Braunstein & Payne, 1968a) that subjects are more sensitive to deviations from right angles than to deviations from acute or obtuse angles. Each subject was assigned to one of two levels of sensitivity to acceleration differences. These levels were the same for both rectangles and trapezoids. The deviation from the frontal plane at which the model made its direction judgments was 36°.

Table 6.1 compares the observed results with those generated by the model. The model accounts for the quantitative differences in the results obtained with rectangles and trapezoids in both studies. Results matched by the model include: (a) the finding of 50% oscillations per cycle for rectangles and 100% for trapezoids with parallel projections; (b) with decreasing projection distance, the more rapid increase to complete accuracy for rectangles than for trapezoids; and (c) the slight increase in accuracy found at intermediate projection distances when the axis of rotation was at the center of the form rather than displaced to one side. (Compare, for example, the symmetric and asymmetric trapezoids at the 1.50 perspective ratio.)

As a further test of the model, an attempt was made to match the result of five other studies (Cook, Mefferd, & Wieland, 1967; Day & Power, 1963; Murch, 1970; Power, 1967; Zegers, 1964), without altering the values of any of the parameters. Each of these studies differed from the first two to which the model was compared in three ways: (a) Subjects observed rotating objects directly, rather than two-dimensional projections of rotating forms. (b) A trial consisted of 20–30 revolutions, as compared to a single revolution in the first two studies. (c) Subjects signalled when they wished to report a reversal of direction, rather than continuously indicating one direction or another. Zegers (1964) presented the most extensive set of quantitative results. Figure 6.8 compares his results with the predictions of the model for an experiment in which reversal frequency was measured as a function of viewing distance. The model follows the observed trend but underestimates reversal frequencies at most distances. This can be attributed to a difference between the

TABLE 6.1

COMPARISONS OF RESPONSE PROPORTIONS GENERATED BY THE MODEL TO OBSERVED PROPORTIONS

	Perspective ratio[a]	Model			Observed		
		Correct	Incorrect	Oscillation	Correct	Incorrect	Oscillation
Symmetric rectangles	1.00[b]	.18	.30	.52	.25	.29	.46
	1.025[c]	.57	.22	.21	.54	.04	.42
	1.051[c]	.61	.17	.22	.58	.08	.33
	1.11[c]	.84	.06	.10	.83	.08	.08
	1.22[c]	.93	.03	.04	1.00	0	0
	1.25[b]	1.00	0	0	.98	.02	0
	1.50[b]	1.00	0	0	1.00	0	0
	1.50[c]	1.00	0	0	1.00	0	0
	1.75[b]	1.00	0	0	1.00	0	0
	2.0[b]	1.00	0	0	.99	0	.01
Asymmetric rectangles	1.025[c]	.57	.10	.33	.58	.08	.33
	1.051[c]	.58	.11	.31	.71	.04	.25
	1.11[c]	.86	.02	.12	.83	0	.17
	1.22[c]	.84	.02	.14	.87	.08	.04
	1.5[c]	1.00	0	0	.92	.04	.04
Symmetric trapezoids	1.025[c]	0	0	1.00	.04	.04	.92
	1.051[c]	.07	0	.93	.17	0	.83
	1.11[c]	.09	0	.91	.08	0	.92
	1.22[c]	.39	0	.61	.46	0	.54
	1.50[c]	.93	0	.07	.92	0	.08
Asymmetric trapezoids	1.00[b]	.03	.03	.94	0	0	1.00
	1.025[c]	0	0	1.00	0	0	1.00
	1.051[c]	.07	0	.93	.08	0	.92
	1.11[c]	.09	0	.91	.04	0	.96
	1.22[b]	.46	0	.54	.31	.03	.66
	1.22[c]	.21	0	.79	.25	0	.75
	1.43[b]	.98	0	.02	.84	.02	.14
	1.50[c]	.78	0	.22	.79	0	.21
	1.64[b]	1.00	0	0	.96	.02	.02
	1.84[b]	1.00	0	0	1.00	0	0

[a] The perspective ratio is the ratio of the sum of the distance of the projection point to the axis of rotation and half the width of the form to the difference between that distance and half the width of the form. A ratio of 1.0 represents a parallel projection (see Braunstein, 1971).

[b] Observed proportions from Braunstein and Payne (1968a). The perspective ratios for the trapezoids in the table are based on the width of the trapezoids and therefore differ from those in the original article which were based on the width of the rectangle used to generate the trapezoids.

[c] Observed proportions from Braunstein (1971).

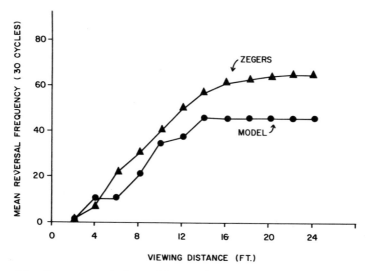

FIGURE 6.8. Comparison of the model to results of Zegers (1964) for variations in viewing distance. [From Braunstein, 1972.]

rotation speed used by Zegers (25 rpm) and that used in the studies on which the parameters of the model are based (8 rpm). Zegers found differences in reversal frequency of this magnitude as a result of differences in rotation speeds in another experiment reported in the same paper. Figure 6.9 compares Zegers' results with the predictions of the model when the length of one of the vertical sides of the form is varied. The rotation speed used by Zegers in the part of his experiment illustrated was 5 rpm. The observed and model results are similar in general trend and in quantitative level.

The model cannot match the quantitative results of Cook, Mefferd, and Wieland (1967). These results are quite different from those of other investigators using similar stimulus materials and viewing distances (e.g., Zegers, 1964; Day & Power, 1963; Power, 1967; Murch, 1970). At a rotation speed of 5 rpm, for example, they obtained 12 times the reversal frequency for a rectangle and twice the frequency for a trapezoid as did Zegers using comparable figure dimensions and viewing distance. Unlike other investigators, Cook et al. failed to find a significant difference between rectangles and trapezoids. These discrepancies may be related to their use of trained rather than naive subjects.

Predictions of the results of other studies preserve the ordinal relationships in the obtained data, although they deviate from the quantitative values reported. For 20 revolutions, mean apparent reversals were obtained of 0 for a rectangle (Day & Power, 1963), 2.9 (Power, 1967),

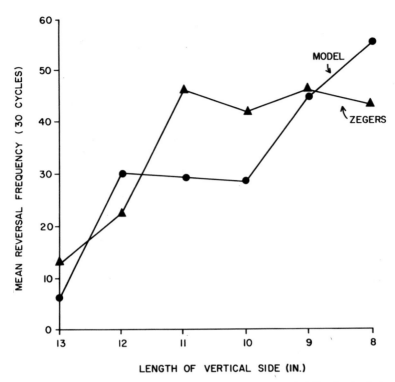

Figure 6.9. Comparison of the model to results of Zegers (1964) for variations in trapezoid dimensions. [From Braunstein, 1972.]

and 3.9 (Murch, 1970) for squares, and 34 (Day & Power, 1963) and 36 (Murch, 1970) for trapezoids. The model predicts means of 2, 4.7, 6.6, 15, and 22, respectively, for the form dimensions and viewing distances used in those studies.

In summary, the model can match the detailed quantitative results of the two studies used to develop it and, without parameter adjustment, can approximate the quantitative findings of the Zegers studies and the qualitative results of other experimenters. The quantitative results obtained with the model depend on subject sensitivity parameters which should be independently measurable. When more data are available on the effects of experimental procedures on these parameters it should be possible to make meaningful parameter adjustments. This should enable the model to fit the quantitative results of a wider variety of experiments. At present, the overall agreement between the ordinal predictions of the model and results obtained in widely differing experimental situations can be regarded as support for this form of model.

Conclusion

There is a fundamental difference between the model presented in this chapter and other explanations that have been offered for the misperception of rotary motion in depth. Each of the explanations previously cited for the rotating trapezoid illusion holds that observers fail to use veridical motion information because this information is weak, absent, or dominated by information from a nonveridical source. In the present theory, the misperception of rotary motion does not involve a conflict between veridical and nonveridical sources of information or the switching from a veridical to a nonveridical source. Instead, the same sources of information and the same processing rules that result in veridical direction judgments for some forms under some viewing conditions are held to result in nonveridical judgments for other forms under other conditions. These sources are related to dynamic changes in the projection of the rotating form rather than to the perception of static characteristics of the form. It seems unlikely that direction judgments would be based on perceptions of static properties of a form that is shown undergoing a continuous transformation. On the contrary, dynamic changes have been shown to be considerably more effective than static properties in determining slant judgments (see Chapter 5). Because the present explanation of nonveridical direction judgments is not based on misperceived initial slant, there is no need to address the question of whether this misperception is due to past experience with windows (Ames, 1951), Gestalt factors (Pastore, 1952), linear perspective (Graham, 1963), or false shape constancy (Gibson & Gibson, 1957).

The model presented in this chapter illustrates the application of process models to the study of depth perception. These are, in essence, models that attempt to be explicit about the sources of information subjects use in judgments and the rules that are applied to information from these sources. The model described here, like process models in a number of other fields of human behavior, relies on heuristic processing rules. The role of heuristic processes in depth perception will be the subject of the final chapter.

7

Heuristic Processes in Perception

AT THE CONCLUSION OF CHAPTER 1, I suggested that the study of visual perception cannot be satisfied with the discovery of sources of information alone, but must identify the processing rules used to combine the relevant information from these sources into perceptual judgments. In subsequent chapters, however, the emphasis remained on the identification of sources of information. This was a reflection of the status of research on depth perception, which has been mainly concerned with describing the relevant stimulus variables. In contrast, the model of the perception of rotary motion presented in the previous chapter was an attempt at formally representing the processing rules used in a perceptual judgment. Hopefully, most of the other judgments described in this book will be so represented in the future, and our knowledge of the nature of perceptual processes will be generally broadened. Our present state of knowledge, however, both in visual perception and in other areas of human cognition, is sufficient for some preliminary comments on the nature of perceptual processes. These processes appear to be heuristic processes, very much like those studied in a variety of areas of human problem solving.

Perception as Problem Solving

Perception has been described by Gregory (1970) as "a kind of problem solving." This is a useful point of view from which to approach the study of perceptual processes. These processes are used to solve a problem that continuously confronts the human or animal observer: transforming information in the optic arrays of the two eyes, combined with information relating to the control of the muscles responsible for accommodation and convergence, into hypotheses concerning the external environment. The hypotheses represent the observer's solutions to the perceptual problem.

Problems are usually thought of as having correct solutions. These correct solutions tend to be defined in a manner external to the solution process. In perception, a correct solution is generally regarded as one that corresponds to physical measurements of the external world. (The term veridical is used synonymously with correct, in this sense.) Perceptual processes should *usually* lead to correct hypotheses about the external world. An evolutionary argument can be made for this postulate (Gibson, 1966, Chap. 1). Perceptual processes that regularly misinformed an animal about his environment would not be expected to be found in species, or individuals, that have survived. Processes do persist, however, that sometimes lead to incorrect perceptions, especially when the perceiver is confronted with an unusual stimulus situation. In other areas of problem solving, there are also processes used that usually lead to correct solutions but occasionally fail to do so. These processes, like perceptual processes, probably fail most often when the problem solver confronts a task environment that is especially different from those he normally faces.

The use of a class of procedures by human subjects that usually, but not always, achieves correct solutions is one of the most important findings in the study of problem solving. These procedures, called heuristic methods, have been described by Simon and Newell (1971) as the central process in human problem solving. The current usage of the term "heuristic" is based on a definition offered by Polya (1945) in the context of theorem proving: "Heuristic reasoning is reasoning not regarded as final and strict but as provisional and plausible only, whose purpose is to discover the solution of the present problem [p. 113]." In the context of problem solving, heuristic processes can be defined as problem-solving methods that tend to produce efficient[1] solutions to difficult problems by

---

[1] The term "efficiency" encompasses various characteristics of the problem-solving process itself as contrasted to the goal of the process, achieving a correct solution.

restricting the search through the space of possible solutions. The restriction on search is based on an evaluation of the structure of the problem.

The same restriction on search that increases efficiency may result in a failure to achieve a correct solution. This characteristic of heuristic methods makes the concept a very difficult one. It seems almost paradoxical that heuristic methods, which are goal oriented procedures that may not achieve their goal, are used in preference to other procedures that are guaranteed to lead to the goal of a correct solution. The preference for heuristic processes appears to be due to their greater efficiency in solving a wide variety of problems. The problem solver sacrifices the certainty of a correct solution for increased efficiency in the solution process.

Heuristic Processes in Problem Solving

Before considering the role of heuristic processes in depth perception, it will be useful to consider examples of this type of information processing in other varieties of human problem solving. There are two reasons for considering other areas of problem solving at this point: First, we can take advantage of the extensive literature on heuristic processes that exists for several other areas of problem solving, in finding illustrations of such concepts as efficiency and restriction of search. Second, we will be able to see some of the similarities that exist between information processing in perception and information processing in the solution of a variety of other problems. The following sections will briefly examine six areas of human problem solving: (*a*) symbolic logic; (*b*) chess; (*c*) pattern recognition; (*d*) binary choice; (*e*) risky decision making; and (*f*) probability estimation. We will consider each area as an illustration of the use of heuristic processes. There is, of course, a great deal more to be said about information processing in problem solving than our purposes here will permit. The reader is referred to Newell and Simon, 1972, for an intensive consideration of this area.

Symbolic Logic

The solution of problems in symbolic logic provides an especially clear illustration of the use of heuristic processes. The problem solver is required to find a sequence of rules that will transform one logic expression into another. An example of such a problem is: transform $R \cdot (\sim P \supset Q)$ into $(Q \vee P) \cdot R$. Examples of rules are $A \cdot B \rightarrow B \cdot A$ and $A \supset B \rightarrow \sim A \vee B$.

Examples of those characteristics will be presented in later sections. In general, the usual meaning of the term, minimization of time and effort, is applicable.

Any sequence of rules that will transform the first expression into the second constitutes a correct solution to the problem.

There is a conceivable solution process that, if carried to completion, guarantees that a correct solution will be achieved. This consists of applying all applicable sequences of rules to the first expression until the second expression is produced. This procedure has been given the name "British Museum Algorithm" after the whimsical observation that "if six chimpanzees were set to work pounding six typewriters at random, they would, in a million years, write all the books in the British Museum [Maloney, 1940]."

The search for a correct solution to a symbolic logic problem can be greatly restricted by making use of the structure of the task environment in the selection of the rules to be applied. Two characteristics of this environment are particularly relevant to the selection of rules: (1) Certain rules reduce certain types of differences between expressions. The rule $A \cdot B \rightarrow B \cdot A$, for example, reduces differences in the positions of variables. (2) Certain rules are directly applicable to certain expressions but not to other expressions. $A \supset B \leftrightarrow \sim A \vee B$, for example, is applicable to $Q \supset R$ but not to $Q \cdot R$. These characteristics of the task environment form the basis for a solution procedure that can be used as an alternative to the British Museum Algorithm:

1. The given expression is compared to the expression to be obtained and the differences between the two expressions are listed. If there is more than one difference, a difference is selected on the basis of a priority ordering of types of differences. Examples of types of differences are: differences in number of variables, in connectives, and in positions of variables. A subgoal is established of reducing the selected difference.

2. The list of rules is searched for a rule applicable to reducing this difference.

3. If a rule is found that is applicable to reducing the difference but is not directly applicable to the current expression, a subgoal is established of making that rule applicable to the current expression. This subgoal, in other words, is one of changing the current expression into one to which the rule is applicable. The subproblem then, like the main problem, is that of changing one expression into another, and steps (1), (2), and (3) may be applied recursively to the subgoal. The subgoal may fail, and another path may be attempted. If one rule cannot be made applicable, for example, another rule may be tried.

This is the essence of the procedure used by the General Problem Solver (Newell, Shaw, & Simon, 1958), a simulation program that appears to accurately represent the heuristic processes used by the human problem solver in solving symbolic logic problems. These processes, which Newell and Simon (1972) refer to as a "means–ends system of heuristic," appear to be generally applicable to task environments consisting of objects (e.g., logic expressions) and operators (e.g., rules), where the goal is one of finding a sequence of operators capable of transforming a given object into a desired one. The heuristic processes in this system include: (1) detecting differences between a given object and a desired one; (2) characterizing operators according to the differences they are able to reduce; (3) modifying an object to make a selected operator applicable; and (4) ordering types of differences between objects according to which differences should be reduced first. Although the use of these processes does not guarantee that the problem at hand will be solved, these processes do succeed for a great many symbolic logic problems. Alternative exhaustive search procedures, such as the British Museum Algorithm, guarantee success but the number of expressions that would have to be searched is so great (Newell & Simon, 1972) that these procedures are not practical for computers and may not even be possible for human problem solvers.

Could the perception of depth through motion be made to fit the General Problem Solver paradigm? The proximal stimulus transformations and the transformations that occur in three-dimensional space could be the objects. The rules of projective geometry that specify the possible relationships between proximal and distal transformations (or, more likely, heuristic approximations to these rules) could be the operators. The goal would be that of finding the original object (the objective motion in three-dimensional space) which gave rise to the available object (the proximal transformation), using the appropriate operators. We are, of course, not dealing with a conscious problem-solving process in the case of depth perception. Still, the analogies between perceptual problem solving and the task environments to which the General Problem Solver is usually applied may be worth considering.

CHESS

There are important similarities between the problem solving task in symbolic logic and that of the chess player. The problem for the chess player is to go from an opening board position to a position in which he wins the game. There is, at least in theory, a complete search procedure available to the player. This consists of considering, for each alternative move, all possible moves of the opponent, all possible responses to those moves, all possible responses of the opponent to those responses, etc., until each path leads to the end of the game. The number of moves that would have to be considered by this complete search procedure far·exceeds the capabilities of either human or machine chess players. In practice, heuristic procedures are used to select among alternative moves. Rather than follow each move to possible ends of the game, the chess player may evaluate alternative moves by an ordered set of questions, such as:

1. Is the king in check?
2. (a) Can material be gained?
   (b) Can material be lost?
   (c) Can material be exchanged?
3. Is castling possible?
4. Can minor pieces be developed? [Bernstein, Arbuckle, de V. Roberts, & Belsky, 1958]

These evaluative questions represent only a small part of the heuristics used in a chess playing program. The behavior of superior chess players is highly complex and still not adequately understood. Progress is being made toward better understanding of these processes through the use of such techniques as verbal protocols (deGroot, 1965) and eye-movement recordings (Tichomirov & Poznyanskaya, 1966).

PATTERN RECOGNITION

Pattern recognition is a type of problem solving that appears simple and commonplace for a person or animal, but is extremely difficult to program for a machine. People appear to use powerful sets of heuristic processes in pattern recognition, processes that still are not understood well enough for machine simulation. The need for heuristic processes in pattern recognition has long been apparent, however, and pattern recognition programs are among the earliest examples of artificial intelligence programs using heuristic processes (Selfridge, 1955; Dineen, 1955). The usual problem in studies of pattern recognition is to go from a two-dimensional array of dark and light areas to the name of one pattern in a set of possible patterns. Recognition of letters of the alphabet from handwriting specimens is a typical example of a pattern recognition problem. The recognition process may be carried out through the use of various measurements of the array, or tests. Even if the set of possible patterns is small, the number of possible tests may be infinite, leaving no conceivable procedure for completely searching the results of all possible tests. Instead, a subset of the possible tests must be elected which usually can correctly distinguish the alternative patterns from one another. Pattern recognition programs may be constructed with a given set of tests that are applied in accordance with their past success (Selfridge & Neisser, 1960), or they may develop their own tests as they are presented with instances of the relevant patterns (Uhr & Vossler, 1961). In either case, the application of these tests represent heuristic processes.

The tests used by a pattern recognition program do not guarantee the correct recognition of every specimen. If the tests are developed for a particular set of specimens, they may well fail when applied to a new specimen that differs markedly from those in the initial set. There has been increasing success in recent years in machine pattern recognition, though the degree to which these programs represent the heuristics used by the human pattern recognizer remains uncertain. A theory of visual perception intended to apply to both human and machine pattern recognition, including the recognition of three-dimensional objects by moving observers, has recently been proposed by Minsky (1975). Minsky's paper is illustrative of an increasing awareness of the relationships between research in both machine and human pattern recognition and research in depth perception. The recognition of three-dimensional objects is a major area of current research in pattern recognition, and though we will not go into further detail on this overlap between the areas of pattern recognition and depth perception here, the reader is referred to Reed (1973) for a review of recent research emphasizing human pattern perception and to Winston (1975) for studies of pattern recognition by computer.

BINARY CHOICE

Symbolic logic, chess, and pattern recognition are tasks that encompass significant artificial intelligence problems. These tasks are difficult for machines, and usually require the use of heuristic procedures. The solution processes used by artificial intelligence devices for these tasks have been of interest as potential models of the solution processes used by people, and the processes used by people have suggested some workable artificial intelligence approaches. It should not be concluded, however, that people use heuristic processes only when alternative procedures that would guarantee a correct solution require the searching of a vast set of alternatives. On the contrary, people use heuristic processes even for problems to which straightforward algorithms, having only a few computational steps, can be applied. The best examples of this behavior come from the study of human judgment, especially in three tasks: binary choice, decision making under risk, and probability estimation. The binary choice problem is among the simplest decision tasks studied, at least in terms of the behavior that would maximize the number of correct responses. A subject is presented a sequence of alternative symbols, such as checks and plusses. The sequence is random, but the probability of each symbol is fixed. When the probability of one symbol is greater than .5, the subject can maximize his number of correct responses by guessing the more frequent symbol on every trial. Subjects characteristically fail to adopt this procedure, tending instead to match their proportion of guesses of each symbol to the probability of that symbol's appearance in the sequence. An analysis of verbal reports collected during trials of a binary choice experiment suggests that subjects use complex heuristic processes directed at finding patterns in the random sequence of alternative symbols (Feldman, 1961). There seems to be an overriding tendency to seek structure in a task environment, even when there is none, and to respond in terms of the supposed structure, even when it is imaginary.

DECISION MAKING UNDER RISK

In another judgmental task, choosing among alternative gambles, people again tend to use heuristic processes rather than straightforward computational algorithms which guarantee an optimal solution. When a probability of winning, probability of losing, amount to be won, and amount to be lost are displayed for each gamble, people appear to choose among gambles on the basis of direct comparisons among these displayed values, rather than on the basis of maximizing expected value. Choices based on the heuristic use of the displayed probabilities and amounts usually correlate well with the choices that would be obtained with expected value maximization, or at least with the maximization of a function of subjective transformations of probability and value, but there are situations in which these heuristics lead to preferences that fail to correspond to those expected from either objective or subjective maximization functions. It has been shown, for example, that people will exhibit consistent preferences among gambles that differ in displayed probabilities and amounts, even when the gambles are mathematically identical and the choice of one over the other can have no objective consequence (Payne & Braunstein, 1971). It has also been shown that the use of displayed probabilities and amounts is not merely due to ignorance of alternative procedures or difficulty in making the required computations. These tendencies persist even after subjects are instructed as to the meaning of expected value and given the expected value of each alternative gamble (Lichtenstein, Slovic, & Zink, 1969).

PROBABILITY ESTIMATION

There is evidence that people use heuristic processes in estimating the probabilities of alternative events (Kahneman & Tversky, 1972, 1973; Tversky & Kahneman, 1973, 1974). Subjects were found to rely on judgmental heuristics even when the information and computational procedures for more accurate probability estimates were available. One of these judgmental heuristics, "availability," results in the relative probability of a class of events' being judged in accordance with the ease with which events in this class come to mind. Tversky and Kahneman (1973) constructed a number of situations in which the most available class of events was not the most probable class. Subjects tended to assign higher estimates of expected frequency to the most available rather than the most probable events. In one situation, subjects were asked to judge whether various consonants (K, L, N, R, and V) appeared more frequently in the first or in the third position in English words. More than two-thirds of the subjects selected the first position as more likely for a majority of the letters, when the third position was in fact more likely for each of the five letters. This was apparently due to the greater ease with which instances of words can be brought to mind when searching by first letter than when searching by third letter.

A second judgmental heuristic is "representativeness." According to this heuristic, people predict the outcome that appears most representative of the situation described. For example, the future occupation of an individual would be predicted on the basis of how well that individual's profile fit the subject's concept of a typical person in that occupation, regardless of such overall statistics as the distribution of people in the population into various occupational categories. This occurred even when the subject was apprised of the low validity of the profile information. Kahneman and Tversky (1972) found that the representativeness heursitic influenced judgments of which of two alternative outcomes was the more likely result of a random process. When asked whether a random distribution of 20 marbles among five children of 4-4-5-4-3 or of 4-4-4-4-4 was more likely, 36 of 52 subjects incorrectly chose the first distribution. The less uniform distribution appeared to better represent their concept of randomness. A number of other examples are presented by these researchers that indicate the importance of both the representativeness and availability heuristics in a wide variety of situations requiring probability estimates. Subjects persisted in their use of these heuristics even when the erroneous nature of their conclusions were explained to them. Tversky and Kahneman (1973, 1974) and Slovic (1972) have discussed the similarity of the persistent judgmental biases that can result from the use of these heuristics to perceptual illusions. This increasing recognition of the similarity of information processing in perception and other judgmental and problem-solving tasks is an important contribution to the understanding of cognitive behavior.

Reasons for Using Heuristic Processes

We have seen that the human problem solver may use processes that do not guarantee a correct solution to the problem at hand. This occurs in a wide variety of problem-solving situations, including: (a) symbolic logic, (b) chess, (c) pattern recognition, (d) binary choice, (e) decision making under risk, and (f) probability estimation. The use of heuristic processes is easy to understand in the first three cases. Even computer programs designed entirely for artificial intelligence purposes have had to use heuristic methods in attempting to solve these problems, because the number of steps required for a complete search of the set of possible solutions would be prohibitive. We can speculate that the human problem solver is forced to use heuristic processes in these cases for similar reasons. In each of the last three cases, however, there is a simple algorithm available that will yield an objectively correct or optimum solution, but people have been found to use heuristic processes instead. There obviously must be compelling reasons for the use of heuristic processes by human problem solvers, in addition to those reasons that usually have motivated their use in artificial intelligence devices. These reasons probably overlap in motivating actual problem solving behavior, but for convenience in discussion they will be separated into four categories: (a) memory limitations, (b) the need or desire for processing speed, (c) the tendency to reduce cognitive strain, and (d) the need to handle degraded information.

MEMORY LIMITATIONS

There are characteristics of human memory that place important limitations on information processing behavior (Newell & Simon, 1972). A well-known example is the limitation of short term memory to "seven, plus or minus two" symbols (Miller, 1956), a restriction that may lead people to use more complex symbols ("chunking") as a means of holding as much information as possible in that memory system. The use of long-term memory is limited by the time and effort required to store symbols. The human problem solver may not be able, within the time available, to store all of the information that might conceivably be required to successfully complete the task at hand, or may not be willing to expend the effort required to do so. Instead, he may use heuristic processes to select the information he considers most likely to be needed later in the task. If later circumstances render the stored information inadequate, the problem solver may fail in the task. Feigenbaum (1961) uses such a partial storage heuristic in his model of paired-associate learning (EPAM). Paired associate learning would be trivial for even the simplest computer, which could store the pairs in coded form and retrieve them with complete accuracy on command. The EPAM model, on the other hand, stores just enough information about a stimulus syllable in a pair to permit retrieval of the correct response at the time of learning. The stored information may become insufficient for the retrieval of the correct response after additional syllable pairs are learned, especially if the new stimulus syllables are similar to the earlier ones. When this happens, EPAM produces retrieval errors much like those attributed to retroactive inhibition in human subjects. This finding, along with other successes of the EPAM model in matching the results of human learning experiments, suggests that the human problem solver uses heuristic processes similar to those found in EPAM to overcome memory limitations.

SPEED

The human problem solver may find it desirable at times to accept some reduction in the probability of achieving a correct solution in order to maximize processing speed. Speed is likely to be a major consideration when adaptive behavior is concerned. Information about a potential threat must be processed fast enough so that a response can be made in time to avoid the threat, even if this means that the identification of the threat will not always be correct. Errors would presumably be biased in favor of unnecessary precautions, or false alarms, when serious threats are involved. Using processes that guaranteed a correct identification of a potential threat, but were too slow for an appropriate response, could be disastrous for the problem solver. A pattern recognition scheme that guaranteed that only lions were recognized as lions might seem more desirable in the abstract than one that mistook other stimuli for lions, but if the former scheme was too slow to allow a person to flee an attacking lion, the scheme (and the person using it) would not be expected to survive.

Speed may be desirable in less dramatic instances. The problem solver must apportion his time among various everyday activities, and he may simply not find it worthwhile to use processes that guarantee correct solutions to everyday problems at the cost of additional processing time. He may find an approximate conceptualization of his spatial environment, for example, quite satisfactory most of the time, even when there is enough information available to the visual system for a more accurate determination of the angles at which various surfaces intersect his line of sight. The time required by processes that used this information might be more than the problem solver is willing to devote to this mundane task.

REDUCING COGNITIVE STRAIN

A heuristic process may be chosen over an alternative process that guarantees a correct solution in order to reduce the mental effort required to solve the problem. The problem solver may be willing to trade some possibility of error for a reduction in cognitive strain. This would occur when the heuristic methods usually provided correct solutions and when there was some acceptable error rate, even if the alternative processes were well within the mental capabilities of the problem solver. Kahneman and Tversky (1972) suggest that reduction in cognitive strain is, in part, the motivation for the use of representativeness and availability heuristics in probability judgments. This could well be the reason for the use of risk dimensions rather than expected value in choices among gambles, and for the use of heuristics in a variety of other judgmental tasks (Payne, 1973).

DEGRADED INFORMATION

There is a final reason for the use of heuristic processes by the human problem solver that is not directly related to overcoming processing limitations or reducing processing effort. The human problem solver often operates in task environments in which the information required by processes capable of guaranteeing a correct solution is incomplete. The probabilities of some or all of the outcomes may not be known to the decision maker, visual pattern recognition may be required in dim illumination, or auditory signal detection may be called for in the presence of background noise. Processes must be used in these situations that can handle degraded information, even if they cannot guarantee a correct solution. This is a possible explanation for the use of heuristic processes under conditions of degraded information. Those heuristic processes that have an advantage in situations of degraded information may also be used when the available information is not degraded. This may occur because people do not find level of information degradation to be a useful criterion for switching processing rules. Instead, for the solution of a particular type of problem, processes are developed that provide some level of resistance to degradation. These processes are then used for undegraded as well as degraded information situations, in preference to alternative processes that would guarantee correct solutions in the undegraded case.

Heuristics and Logical Consistency

The preceding sections considered possible reasons for the use of heuristic processes by human problem solvers. These reasons appear to outweigh the principal disadvantage of heuristic processes: their failure to guarantee that a correct solution to the problem will be reached. There is a secondary difficulty arising from the use of heuristic processes which should be made explicit. The use of these processes sometimes results in judgments that are not logically consistent. Different types of judgments about the same stimuli, which should be logically related, may prove contradictory because different heuristics are applied to each type of judgment. This does not seem to present serious difficulties for the problem solver, but it does present a challenge to the behavioral scientist seeking consistent underlying principles that can explain observed behavior.

A particularly striking example of inconsistent judgments about the same stimuli comes from a study of risky decision making. Lichtenstein and Slovic (1971) asked the same subjects to make two different types of judgments about the same simple gambles: bids and choices. In the bid judgments, subjects stated the amount of money that they would be willing to pay for the privilege of playing each gamble. In the choice situation, the gambles were presented in pairs and the subjects indicated which member of each pair they would prefer to play. It was not unusual for a subject to bid more for one of two gambles in the bid portion of the experiment, and to choose the other gamble when the two gambles were presented as a pair in the choice portion. Even when directly confronted with the inconsistencies in their judgments in post-experimental interviews, some subjects persisted in these inconsistencies. Subjects displaying inconsistent behavior appeared to be using different heuristics in the two types of judgments, in that the amounts were emphasized in bid judgments and the probabilities were emphasized in choice judgments.

There is a similar logical inconsistency in two types of perceptual judgments involved in the well-known moon illusion. Consider the Rock and Kaufman (1962) explanation of this illusion: The horizon moon is perceived as more distant than the zenith moon (probably due to contour convergence in the foreground terrain). As both moons subtend the same visual angle, and size judgments are assumed to be a function of visual angle and perceived distance, the horizon moon is judged to be larger. When asked to judge the distance of the horizon moon relative to the zenith moon, however, subjects tend to judge the horizon moon to be closer, possibly because it appears larger. This explanation was disputed by Boring (1962) because it appeared to describe a perceptual process that is not logically consistent. Dees (1966) questioned the appropriateness of a criterion of logical consistency, stating that "most 'perceptual logic' is subverbal and in large measure automatic and based upon learned premises which usually are true." This statement is quite consistent with the present theory of heuristic perceptual processes.

Heuristic Processes in Depth Perception

The term "heuristic" is not as common in the literature on depth perception as it is in writings in other areas of problem solving, but a number of perceptual judgments have been studied that reflect heuristic processes. Two such judgments, relative distance and absolute distance, have been examined in detail by Gogel (1973a,b). There appears to be a process underlying relative distance judgments that produces judgments of equidistance when two or more objects are presented under conditions of reduced distance information. Gogel refers to this effect as the equidistance tendency. A second process can be inferred from judgments of the absolute distance of an object or surface presented under similar conditions of reduced distance information. Subjects tend to attribute a specific distance to the object or surface. This behavior is referred to by Gogel as the specific distance tendency. The perceptual processes reflected in these two tendencies, like other heuristic processes, may result in incorrect judgments. Relative distance judgments will be incorrect when the objects are not equidistant. Absolute distance judgments will be incorrect if the actual distance does not correspond to that favored by the specific distance tendency. When distance information is totally removed from the stimulus situation, these processes can be regarded as guessing procedures, and their failure to achieve accurate judgments of relative and absolute distance would be of little interest. The equidistance and specific distance tendencies, however, have been shown to persist even when the optic array contains sufficient information for veridical distance judgments. The use of these processes, under such conditions, may reduce the level of accuracy of distance judgments from that level that could potentially be achieved with the information in the optic array.

Another example of the use of a heuristic process in depth perception is found in the judgment of degree of slant for a stationary surface, discussed in Chapter 5. These judgments are made principally on the basis of the pattern of converging lines in the retinal projection, or of converging texture elements if lines are not explicitly present. The pattern of converging lines, however, does not necessarily provide a correct indication of surface slant. Of three stimulus conditions under which slant judgments have been studied, the pattern of converging lines always contains veridical information about surface slant under one condition, sometimes does so under another, and rarely does so under a third. The first condition is the direct observation of a surface containing parallel lines that are perpendicular to the axis of rotation. In this condition, surface slant is equal to a function of the pattern of converging lines and a visual angle subtended by a part of the pattern. The second condition is the observation of an artificial projection of a surface of the type specified above. Artificial projections include paintings, photographs, and views through magnifying and demagnifying lenses. Correct slant judgments based on the pattern of converging lines are possible in artificial projections only when the distance at which the projection is viewed is equivalent to the distance between the projection point and the projection plane in the optical system used to generate the projection. The third condition involves the perception of a surface that contains converging rather than parallel lines or converging texture elements rather than uniformly spaced elements. Judgments of surface slant based on the pattern of converging lines in the retinal projection of that surface would generally be misleading. An example of this is the misperception of slant in a stationary trapezoid (Smith, 1967). In most of these stimulus situations there is an alternative source of information that would always provide veridical information about surface slant: form ratio (see Chapter 5). If subjects judged slant on the basis of form ratio, their judgments would be accurate regardless of whether the projected image were magnified or demagnified. If the texture elements were identifiable in the projection of a slanted surface, and the spacing of these elements in the original texture were known, slant judgments based on form ratio would be accurate regardless of whether the texture density was uniform or the contour lines were parallel. Experimental evidence, however, shows that subjects use the pattern of converging lines to judge degree of slant in stationary views of regular patterns when that source of information and form ratio are placed in conflict. (Braunstein & Payne, 1969).

Heuristic Processes in the Perception of Rotary Motion

The two principal processing rules incorporated in the model of the perception of rotary motion, described in the preceding chapter, are examples of heuristic processes. The first decision rule produces judgments that a side of a quadrilateral is approaching when the angles that include that side decrease and, conversely, that a side is receding when the contour angles increase. This rule will always produce correct judgments, assuming detectable angle changes, if the angles of the distal object are right angles. It will also produce correct judgments whenever the object is sufficiently close, regardless of the angle sizes in the distal object. The range of viewing distances at which this rule produces correct judgments depends on the angle sizes and other dimensions in the distal object. For objects having other than right angles between contours, there are distances at which this decision rule will produce systematic errors in judgment. These errors are especially consistent for trapezoids.

There is an alternative rule that would always produce correct judgments of direction of rotation when the information it requires is detectable. This rule would simply require that a side be judged as approaching when its projection on the retina increases and that a side be judged as receding when its projection decreases. This rule would yield correct judgments regardless of contour angle, as long as the object was not so distant as to render changes in the projected size undetectable. Despite the potential of this rule based on projected size to produce accurate judgments in all situations, the contour angle rule, which makes systematic errors for such figures as trapezoids, is preferred.

The second heuristic processing rule in the model produces judgments of approach on the basis of the relative acceleration of two contours. If the rotation is about a vertical axis, the more rapidly accelerating vertical side is judged to be approaching. This rule can produce accurate judgments when the vertical sides in the distal object are equidistant from the axis of rotation, so long as the difference in acceleration is detectable. If the vertical sides are not equidistant from the axis of rotation, and the viewing distance is sufficiently great, this rule can produce systematic errors in direction of rotation judgments. Yet this rule contributes to direction judgments even when an alternative rule based on changes in the projections of the same two sides could form the basis for accurate judgments, regardless of whether the sides are equidistant from the axis of rotation.

Why are heuristic processes used to determine direction of rotation when there is a simple algorithm that would guarantee a correct judgment? Possible reasons were given earlier for the use of heuristic processes under such circumstances for problem solving in general. These included limitations in memory capabilities, a need to process information rapidly, a tendency to minimize cognitive strain, and a need to handle degraded information. At this point we can only speculate as to which of these reasons apply to the present case. There does not appear to be a memory problem involved in the use of the alternative algorithm that was suggested above for judging direction of rotation. Determining whether a continuously changing projection of a contour is increasing or decreasing does not, a priori, seem to produce a greater load on memory than determining whether a projected contour angle is increasing or decreasing. The remaining possibilities appear plausible as reasons for the use of heuristic processes in judgments of rotary motion. In particular, the need for speed and the need to handle degraded information suggest empirical studies which may shed additional light on the role of heuristic processes in depth perception. For this reason, these two possibilities will be considered in detail.

The possibility that heuristic processes are used to increase the speed of direction-of-rotation judgments implies that the heuristic rules require less processing time than that required by alternative processes that guarantee correct judgments. Specifically, the implication is that angle changes

A second similarity between the present approach and that of J. J. Gibson is concerned with the more specific question of what type of information in the optic array determines the perception of three-dimensional space. Both approaches emphasize higher-order variables. Gibson has shown the importance of gradients in the optic array (1946) and particularly of transformations of the optic array (1957) as stimuli for the perception of three-dimensional space, and the present approach rests heavily on his pioneering efforts.

A third similarity is in the explicit recognition of the importance of adaptation to an environment in the determination of an organism's perceptual capabilities. This is considered in detail by Gibson (1966). Adaptation is considered here as a possible explanation for the selection of one perceptual process over another, especially when a heuristic process, which does not guarantée a correct solution, is preferred to a process that does.

It is on this last point, the use of heuristic processes, that the present approach differs from Gibson's. Gibson states that his theory is "primarily a theory of correct perception [that] must explain incorrect perception by supplementary assumptions [1966, p. 287]." The present approach holds that both correct and incorrect perception must be explained by the same processes, and is concerned with showing why processes are used by the human observer that sometimes fail to yield correct perceptions.

The second difference between Gibson's approach and the present one follows from Gibson's emphasis on correct perception. Gibson's theory holds that correct perception results from the use of invariants in the optic array in perceptual judgments. In his theory, the role assigned to processes based on invariants is very much like that of algorithms that guarantee correct solutions in other areas of problem solving: As long as the information required to calculate the invariant properties of a stimulus are available to the observer, perception should be correct. People do not seem to use processes based on invariants, however, in actual perceptual judgments. They use heuristic processes instead. These usually, although not always, yield judgments indistinguishable from those that would result from the use of invariants. When correct perceptual judgments are obtained, there may be no way to tell whether a heuristic process or a process based on an invariant was used in these judgments. When systematic illusions occur, it may be easy to show that heuristic processes were responsible. Demonstrating that the same processes underlie both correct perceptions and systematic illusions is more difficult. It requires a research strategy in which stimulus conditions are varied between those that yield correct perception and those that maximize a particular illusion. If the same heuristic processes can predict the entire range of results, this tends to support the theory that these processes form the basis for correct as well as illusory perception. This is the approach described in Chapter 6 as the basis for a model of the perception of rotary motion. The same heuristic processes were used to explain both the accurate perception of rotary motion, found for rectangles, and the systematic illusion of oscillation, found for trapezoids.

Additional evidence for the use of heuristic processes rather than processes based on invariants is found in the greater weight given to perspective than to form ratio in judgments of the slant of static surfaces. The use of perspective is a heuristic that does not guarantee accurate slant judgments, while form ratio is an invariant from which surface slant can always be derived when the required information is present.

It is possible to begin an analysis of depth perception by enumerating the available invariants on which depth judgments might be based and then considering the ways in which people deviate from the use of these invariants, but a better strategy would be one of looking directly for the heuristic processes that people actually use. There has been an analogous situation in the study of decision making. Much of the earlier research in that area was concerned with the ways in which people deviated from normative decision rules, such as maximization of expected value, and normative probability estimation rules, such as the Bayesian model. Marked progress has been made in the study of human decision making in recent years as a result of a direct interest in discovering the heuristic processes that people actually use in making decisions and in estimating probabilities.

JOHANSSON

Johansson (1970), in a critique of Gibson's (1966) writings concerning "ecological optics," sketches a theoretical structure that stresses the analysis of the proximal stimulus by the visual system. This is contrasted to Gibson's emphasis on the relationship between the distal environment and the information available about this environment at the eye. Johansson holds that the visual system derives its efficiency from the application of a set of rules or "decoding principles" that work in a "blind, mechanical way" when applied to the proximal stimulus. He uses the programming of a computer as an analogy, comparing the adaptability found at higher levels of the visual system to the possibility of changing some instructions and constants to modify the outputs of a computer program. The present approach is in general agreement with these concepts, although there is a difference in the type of rules, or perceptual processes, sought by Johansson and his coworkers and the heuristic processes proposed here.

Johansson's approach stresses the computational possibilities that proximal stimulus information presents to the visual system. A vector analysis is typically used to define the geometrically possible three-dimensional stimuli from which the proximal stimulus could arise, and subjects' responses are compared to these possibilities. The type of rules implied by this approach are rules that remain faithful to the projective geometry of the stimulus situation, a property not necessarily incorporated in the heuristic rules proposed here. This is an important difference in the two approaches, but the similarities in emphasizing dynamic properties of the proximal stimulus and in seeking processes that relate the proximal stimulus to perception are even more significant.

Conclusion

The theory presented here of the heuristic nature of perceptual processes has some very specific implications for future research in depth perception, and perhaps for perceptual research generally. We have already examined one implication: Research on perceptual judgments must be concerned with discovering underlying processes, not merely with identifying relevant sources of information. There are two remaining implications that follow from the heuristic nature of perceptual processes. The first of these implications is that we should not, in our effort to understand perceptual processes, limit our consideration to processes that necessarily lead to correct perception. The requirements of correct perception should be kept in mind, because perception is usually in correspondence with the physical environment. We must recognize, however, that this usual correctness may be based on heuristic processes which produce judgments that tend to correlate well with those that would be produced by processes guaranteeing correctness, but which are really very different processes. The study of the geometry of the stimulus situation should not dominate our thinking about perceptual processes, lest our theories be geometrically sophisticated but psychologically naive.

A corollary of this implication is that the identification of relevant sources of information should not be limited to those sources that can yield correct judgments. More precisely, it should not be limited to sources that are useable by processes yielding geometrically correct judgments. This point was made earlier in connection with theories based on invariants. The actual sources of information used by perceptual processes may not be invariant under all conditions of observation, and processes based on these sources may yield correct judgments sometimes and incorrect judgments, or illusions, at other times. This leads to our final implication: The study of illusions is of major importance to the understanding of perceptual processes.

A fundamental tenet of the theory proposed here is that the same perceptual processes lead to both veridical perceptions and illusions. The occurrence of systematic illusions does not imply that these processes are malfunctioning. On the contrary, they are being applied in a normal manner to a stimulus situation that is not among those for which the processes yield correct judgments. The situation is like that of the problem solver faced with a particular symbolic logic problem for which his heuristic search procedure will never uncover the correct path. Another analogous situation would be a computer program's production of incorrect output because the input data is not in the range for which it can produce accurate results. The program is operating correctly, i.e., it is executing its instructions as they exist in the computer, and the computer is not malfunctioning, yet the output is incorrect when judged by an external standard. Similarly, an illusion does not represent a malfunction of perceptual processes, but rather the normal functioning of processes that are not designed to produce veridical judgments in all situations.

If illusions reflect the same processes that lead to veridical perception, they should provide a key to our understanding of these processes. As Leibowitz (1965) has pointed out, an unexplained illusion should "be considered an indication that our knowledge of fundamental laws of perception is inadequate [p. 42]." There are often many alternative processes that could equally well account for veridical perception, but far fewer that could also explain particular illusions. To return to the computer program analogy, there may be many programs that will perform the same over-all operation, such as a statistical analysis, and correct results may tell us little about how a particular program operates. If the program makes a peculiar error when given unusual inputs, however, we may be able to make some promising inferences about its internal processes.

Without the little man in the eye to help us avoid the issue of perceptual processing, we must formulate theories of perception that trace the processing rules from the information in the proximal stimulus to the resulting perceptual judgments. With these rules understood as heuristic processes, greater progress should be possible in the discovery of particular processing rules and in the assembly of these rules into general theories of visual perception.

Appendix:
Computer Animation

A MAJOR PORTION OF THE research described in this book on the role of transformations in depth perception used the technique of computer animation. The equipment required for computer animation is now widely available. There are well-documented software packages in FORTAN, BASIC, and other higher-level computer languages. Any researcher or student of visual perception should be able to explore this technique as a means of generating either some of the stimulus materials discussed in this book or new materials of interest. This appendix is intended to assist those who would like to try computer animation. Some knowledge of programming would be helpful to the reader, but this is not essential. The reader without programming skills will be able to follow all but the specific programming examples, and even these should not be hard to figure out.

Graphic Displays

The essential hardware in a computer animation system is a graphic display. This is a cathode ray tube (CRT), not unlike a television picture tube in appearance and general functioning. The surface area of the tube might be thought of as a sheet of graph paper. A typical display might have a resolution of 1024 plotting positions on each axis. This means that the lower left point on the surface of the tube is represented in the animation system as having the coordinates (0,0), and the upper right point has coordinates (1023,1023). The point (512,512) is near the center of the tube's surface. The basic idea behind a graphic display is that a point (actually a spot of light) can be made to appear anywhere on the surface of a cathode ray tube by specifying the X and Y coordinates, just as you would plot a point on a sheet of graph paper by finding the X and Y coordinates of that point. In computer graphics, the coordinates are specified as part of the operation of a computer program. The cathode ray tube is an output device for the computer. Just as the computer might be commanded to print a number on its high-speed printer, type a word at a teletype, or punch a hole in a card, it can be commanded to plot a point at coordinates (X,Y) on a CRT. In many systems, an alternative command is to draw a line from (X1,Y1) to (X2,Y2). More complex displays can be constructed from these points and lines.

REFRESH VERSUS STORAGE DISPLAYS

There are many types of graphic displays, but for our present purposes only two major distinctions will be considered: refresh versus storage displays, and on-line versus off-line displays. Each cathode ray tube is coated with phosphorescent material. When a command is issued to plot a point at a given pair of X,Y coordinates, a beam of light is directed to that location on the surface of the tube and a spot will phosphoresce at that location. The duration of this phosphorescence is a characteristic of the particular coating used on the tube. Refresh displays are characterized by rapid decay of the phosphor. The spot may, for example, be visible for only one-hundredth of a second. If a longer display time is desired with a refresh display, the beam must be directed at the spot once again, producing a new period of phosphorescence. This is referred to as refreshing the display, and is the basis for the display's designation. Storage displays have very slow phosphor decay periods. Once a spot is illuminated in a storage display it usually will continue to phosphoresce until a specific action is taken to erase the entire display. The erase procedure involves a brief increase in the brightness of the entire scope. There is a delay of about a second before a new display can be plotted.

There are advantages and disadvantages of refresh and storage displays which follow from the characteristics just described. The refresh display is especially useful when spots must be presented for brief periods. A point could be shown in apparent motion, for example, by displaying spots successively in different positions. This could be done against a constant background if desired, by refreshing the background often enough to avoid flicker, while the spot is allowed to disappear at each position and to later reappear at a new position along the apparent motion path. This is possible because the refresh display allows separate computer control of the display time of each individual spot. But this flexibility has its price: The computer must keep track of every spot that is to be displayed for longer than the phosphor decay time, and must transmit this information to the display at these brief intervals. This means that a considerable amount of computing power and high speed storage is tied up by a refresh display. Often, the entire capabilities of a laboratory computer must be dedicated to controlling a single refresh display. Some displays of this type are available with their own built-in minicomputers, as well as facilities for communication with a general purpose computer which can handle the over-all display generation program (Reddy, Rosen, Kriz, Powell, & Broadley, 1975).

The storage display requires relatively little computer capacity, because the computer does not keep track of each spot in the display. Once a spot is caused to phosphoresce it remains in that state until the display is erased. No further communication from the computer is necessary. Modern minicomputers can simultaneously control a number of storage displays, each display presenting different information to the user. The disadvantage of the storage display is in the erase procedure. A single spot cannot be made to disappear; the display must be erased totally if any part of it is to be deleted. A moving spot cannot be displayed against a constant background, unless the background is redrawn after each erasure of the spot. Apparent motion cannot be displayed because of the delay required between the erasure of the current display and the plotting of a new one. In summary, the refresh display requires considerable computer capacity but can display apparent motion; the storage display requires relatively little computer capacity but cannot directly display apparent motion.

ON-LINE VERSUS OFF-LINE DISPLAYS

In comparing refresh and storage displays, we have been concerned primarily with on-line displays. These displays are attached to computers, which determine the positions at which points or lines are to be plotted and cause them to appear on the face of the cathode ray tube in real time. A great deal of animation work has been accomplished with off-line displays. In an off-line system, the computer does not produce the display directly but produces a set of coded commands, usually writing these on magnetic tape. The tape is then taken to a microfilm plotter that produces the display on the basis of the coded commands. The microfilm plotter contains a cathode ray tube with a rapidly decaying phosphor. The tube is photographed by a camera that is also controlled by the coded commands. When the camera shutter opens, each spot in the display phosphoresces long enough to be recorded on film and then disappears. When the display is complete, the shutter is closed and the film is advanced. A principal advantage of this off-line system is that the displays can be produced at a central facility which may have far more precise cathode ray tube displays and camera equipment than can be made available in an individual laboratory. The disadvantages are in the extra time required for the two-step procedure of first producing a magnetic tape and later generating the display, and the costs that may be incurred in the use of a specialized microfilm plotter facility.

Setting Up an Animation Laboratory

Of the types of displays described, the most widely available is the on-line storage display. It is not coincidental that this is the easiest display to program. It is probably also the most economical for computer animation. Our major concern will therefore be with the on-line storage display. On-line refresh displays and off-line microfilm plotters are also widely used in perceptual research, and will be considered later.

On-line storage displays are available as parts of general purpose computer terminals. They usually come with standard keyboards and with interfaces for connection to any computer that communicates with teletypes or similar terminals. As an example of a graphic display terminal, consider the Tektronix 4010, shown in Figure A.1. This terminal will function in an "alphanumeric" mode, displaying numbers and letters line by line. It will also operate in a graphic mode, displaying points or lines at specified coordinates. In the graphic mode, the lower left corner of the screen has the coordinates $(0,0)$ and the upper right has the coordinates $(1023,780)$.

The use of the 4010 or similar graphic display terminal for animation is straightforward. A motion picture camera is placed in front of the terminal (see Figure A.1). The points and lines to be included in the first frame of the motion picture are plotted. The camera, which must be operable in a single frame mode, records the display on one frame of film and advances the film to the next frame. The display is then erased and the next frame is plotted and photographed. This process continues until all of the frames in the motion picture have been recorded on film. The process is necessarily a slow one, because of the time required to

FIGURE A.1.   The principal components of a computer animation laboratory.

erase each display and advance the camera. One second in the final motion picture, 24 frames, may take two minutes or longer to photograph. Fortunately, the procedure is easily automated. This requires a camera with a motor drive that can be pulsed in a single frame mode, under computer control. (We have been using Lafayette Instrument's Model K-100.) It is possible to wire the camera control unit to the graphic display terminal or to a relay driver on the computer, if one is available. We have found it more convenient to use a voice-actuated relay. A microphone is taped over the bell (actually a speaker emitting a tone) on the 4010 terminal. The microphone is connected to the voice-actuated relay unit. The external pulsing contacts of the camera control unit are wired across the normally open contacts of the voice-actuated relay. The camera can then be pulsed by commanding the bell to ring on the terminal. This eliminates the need to actually wire the computer or terminal to the camera control unit.

If a refresh display is to be used instead of a storage display, a camera may not be used at all. Subjects may be asked to observe the display itself as it produces apparent movement in real time. This method usually limits the amount of material that can be displayed because of the computer capacity required by refresh displays. Refresh displays can be photographed to produce animated motion pictures, just as can storage displays. It may be necessary, however, to synchronize the camera with the refresh cycle of the display so that all parts of the display are at the same brightness when the frame is recorded.

Off-line displays are photographed frame-by-frame, like storage displays.

The user of these displays does not have to be concerned with the camera setup because this is a part of the microfilm plotter, although it may be necessary to specify the film type required, e.g., 16 mm with sprocket holes. It may also be necessary to specify that the frames are to be photographed in the "cine" mode rather than in the "comic" mode. The former mode means that the top of one frame borders on the bottom of the adjacent frame, as in a motion picture. In the latter mode, intended for microfilm readers, the frames are side by side, as in a comic strip.

Computational Procedures

The computations required for using computer animation to study the role of transformations in depth perception come from solid trigonometry and analytical geometry. Green (1958) has described the applicable formulas, and the following presentation rests heavily on his description.

We can conveniently separate the computational procedures into three parts: (1) generating the figure, (2) transforming the figure in three-dimensional space, and (3) projecting the transformed figure onto a plane.

GENERATING THE FIGURE

If the figure is to be a line drawing, such as a rectangle or a trapezoid, the coordinates may be provided as input to the program or as data within the program. For example, the points $(-.6,.7)$, $(-.6,-.7)$, $(.6,-.5)$, $(.6,.5)$, specify a trapezoid. The program need only connect the points in sequence, and connect the last point to the first. Note that we are using coordinates in the range of -1 to $+1$. This is convenient for internal computations. When the final display is calculated, the coordinates can be converted back to the range of 0 to 1023, or to whatever system is required for the graphic display.

Random dot figures are usually generated from equations within the program. As a first example, consider dots to be placed within the confines of an unseen square, having sides of length 2 and centered at $(0,0)$. Let RND be a random number between 0 and 1. (RND is a different number each time it appears in an.equation.) We would then select the coordinates of the points in the display by:

$$X = 2*RND - 1$$
$$Y = 2*RND - 1,$$

where * indicates multiplication. If the dots are to fall instead within a circle of unit radius, centered at (0,0), we could use the following equations:

$$T = 2*PI*RND$$
$$R = SQR(RND)$$
$$X = R*COS(T)$$
$$Y = R*SIN(T),$$

where PI is the constant π and SQR means square root. This procedure randomly selects an angle (T) and radius (R) and then converts from polar to Cartesian coordinates. The square root function is used in order to maintain a uniform distribution of dots, as the area to be filled in a circle increases with the square of the radius. Alternatively, we could use the first set of equations to locate the points in a square and then reject all points for which

$$X**2 + Y**2 > 1,$$

where ** indicates exponentiation. This would leave only those points that fell within the inscribed circle.

The examples presented thus far have involved two-dimensional figures. The Z coordinates of each point are assumed to be 0. Consider now a three-dimensional random dot pattern. The dots will be confined to an unseen sphere of unit radius, centered at (0,0,0). A procedure for filling the sphere with dots can be extrapolated from the procedure described for the circle. In the case of the sphere, two angles (T and Q) and a radius (R) must be randomly selected:

$$T = 2*PI*RND$$
$$Q = PI*RND$$
$$R = RND**(\frac{1}{3}).$$

The cube root of a random number is used for the radius because the volume to be filled varies with the cube of the radius. The Cartesian coordinates are given by:

$$X = R*SIN(T)*COS(Q)$$
$$Y = R*COS(T)$$
$$Z = R*SIN(T)*SIN(Q).$$

Unfortunately, these formulas do not give altogether satisfactory results because the dots concentrate at the poles of the sphere. The simplest way to avoid this is to generate the points uniformly in a cube and reject those that do not fall within the inscribed sphere:

$$X = 2*RND - 1$$
$$Y = 2*RND - 1$$
$$Z = 2*RND - 1.$$

Points are then rejected if $X**2 + Y**2 + Z**2 > 1$.

TRANSFORMING THE FIGURE

Because our objective is to produce a motion picture of a transforming pattern, we must decide on the type of transformation to be displayed and on how much motion is to occur on each frame. If the type of motion is to be a translation along X, Y, or Z axis, we simply add an increment to the appropriate coordinate for each frame. To cause a group of dots to move from left to right, a positive increment would be added to the X coordinate of each dot. The Y and Z coordinates would be left unchanged. If the dots are to move by one unit (we are still using arbitrary units at this point) in 72 frames, the increment would be 1/72. The critical problem in translations is to keep the pattern from disappearing. The pattern has to be large enough in the dimension of the translation so that it doesn't leave the field of view. A pattern to be translated along the X axis, for example, would best be in the shape of a long rectangle or cylinder rather than a square, circle, or sphere. The formula for translation along the X axis is:

$$X = X1 + I,$$

where I is the increment and X1 is the X coordinate of the point on the previous frame. An alternative computational procedure is:

$$X = X0 + F*I,$$

where X0 is the initial X coordinate and F is the frame number.

If a rotation is to be displayed about the X, Y, or Z axis, the angle of rotation per frame must be determined. For a 360° (i.e., 2*PI) rotation to be displayed in N frames, the angle per frame would be 2*PI/N. The formulas for rotation about the Y axis are:

$$X = X1*COS(T) + Z1*SIN(T)$$
$$Z = Z1*COS(T) - X1*SIN(T),$$

where X1 and Z1 are the X and Z coordinates of the point on the previous frame and T is the angle of rotation per frame. There is no change in the coordinate corresponding to the axis of rotation, the Y coordinate in this case. An alternative computational procedure is:

$$X = X0*COS(T*F) + Z0*SIN(T*F)$$
$$Z = Z0*COS(T*F) - X0*SIN(T*F),$$

where X0 and Z0 are the initial X and Z coordinates and F is the frame number. This procedure is especially convenient if the initial pattern is two-dimensional because all Z0 coordinates will then be zero, and those terms that include Z0 as a factor will drop out. These formulas can, of course, be generalized to other orthogonal axes or to oblique axes.

PROJECTING THE FIGURE

We have now reviewed the procedures for generating a figure and for translating or rotating that figure. With a few exceptions (two-dimensional figures translating along the X or Y axes or rotating about the Z axis), the transformation will take place in three dimensions. The final step in computer animation is, therefore, projecting the three-dimensional pattern computed for each frame of the motion picture onto a two-dimensional plane, so that it can be plotted on the face of a cathode ray tube. If a parallel projection is to be used, we simply ignore the Z coordinates and plot the X and Y coordinates. A polar projection is most conveniently computed by placing the projection plane through the origin, at $Z = 0$. (The position of the projection plane affects the scale of the display only. The scale is arbitrary in the computational procedure. It is ultimately determined when the motion picture is projected onto a screen.) The selection of the projection point is of great consequence in the generation of a polar projection, because the distance of the projection point determines the amount of perspective in the display, as defined, for example, by the perspective ratio (see Chapter 4). The formulas for polar projection are:

$$X2 = X*E/(E{-}Z)$$
$$Y2 = Y*E/(E{-}Z),$$

where X2 and Y2 are the projected coordinates corresponding to the point (X,Y,Z), and E is the distance of the projection point from the origin, i.e., the projection point is at (0,0,E).[1]

---

[1] The subject's viewing distance can be made to correspond to the projection point distance by measuring a projection plane unit on the screen when the motion picture is projected and using that measurement to convert the projection distance to a viewing distance. Consider a display computed with the projection plane at $Z=0$ and the projection point 3 units from the origin, for example. A projection plane unit could be defined by a line drawn on the projection plane from (0,0) to (1,0). Let us say that this line measures .5m on the screen when the film is projected. The subject's viewing distance would have to be set to 1.5m, to match the 3-unit projection point distance used in the computations.

Programming Example

We will now consider a specific programming example, a six-frame sequence displaying rotation about the Y axis of 100 dots randomly located within the confines of a sphere (Table A.1). The language is BASIC-PLUS, available on various models of the PDP-11. The graphic functions are part of a package written by the author for the Tektronix 4010. Packages that include similar functions are available for use with FORTRAN for a number of other computers. (A description and listing of the complete graphics package are available from the author.) The sample program uses the following graphic functions:

FNG (i, j)

Sets parameters in the graphics package.
Example: Z = FNG (0,0) initializes the package.

FNG3 (X1, Y1, X2, Y2)

Defines an arbitrary coordinate system for use in the program.
Example: Z = FNG3 ($-1, -1, 1, 1$) specifies an internal coordinate system from (-1, -1) at the lower left to ($+1, +1$) at the upper right.

FNG4 (U1, V1, U2, V2)

Specifies the portion of the scope (in scope coordinates) to be occupied by the internal coordinate system defined by FNG3.
Example: Z = FNG4 (100, 100, 700, 700), if preceded by the FNG3 call in the previous example, would cause the internal coordinates ($-1, -1$) to appear at scope coordinates (100, 100), and ($+1, +1$) to appear at (700, 700), with intermediate coordinates appropriately scaled.

FNG6 (i)

Executes various control functions.
Example: Z = FNG6 (1) erases the screen and pauses.

FNG7 (x, y, i)

Plots points (and lines).
Example: Z = FNG7 (.5, $-.4$, 1) plots a point at (.5, $-.4$). The X and Y values are in the internal coordinate system.

TABLE A.1
SAMPLE COMPUTER ANIMATION PROGRAM

```
100  Z=FNG(0,0)                ! GRAPHICS INITIALIZATION
110  Z=FNG3(-1,-1,1,1)         ! LIMITS OF YOUR COORDINATE SYSTEM
120  Z=FNG4(150,50,830,        ! AREA OF SCOPE TO WHICH YOUR
     730)                          COORDINATE SYSTEM CORRESPONDS

140  DIM X0(100),
     Y0(100),Z0(100)          ! DIMENSIONS FOR INITIAL POINTS
200  E=3                       ! VIEWING DISTANCE WILL BE 3 UNITS
                                   FROM THE ORIGIN
210  M=6                       ! SIX FRAMES ARE TO BE PRODUCED
220  T=2*PI/M                  ! ANGLE OF ROTATION PER FRAME
230  N=100                     ! THERE WILL BE 100 POINTS
                                 IN THE DISPLAY
240  FOR I=1 TO N              ! POINTS IN A SPHERE
250  X0(I)=2*RND-1             ! X COORDINATE
260  Y0(I)=2*RND-1             ! Y COORDINATE
270  Z0(I)=2*RND-1             ! Z COORDINATE
280  IF X0(I)**2+
     Y0(I)**2+Z0(I)**2
     > 1 THEN 250              ! POINT REJECTED IF OUTSIDE UNIT
                                   SPHERE
290  NEXT I                    ! END OF FIGURE GENERATION LOOP
300  FOR F=1 TO M              ! FRAME LOOP
310  S=SIN(T*F)                ! SIN OF CURRENT ANGLE
320  C=COS(T*F)                ! COS OF CURRENT ANGLE
330  FOR I=1 TO N              ! POINT LOOP (WITHIN FRAME LOOP)
340  X=X0(I)*C+Z0(I)*S         ! Y ROTATION, FIRST PART
350  Z=Z0(I)*C-X0(I)*S         ! Y ROTATION, SECOND PART
360  Y=Y0(I)                   ! NO CHANGE IN Y
370  X2=X*E/(E-Z)              ! PROJECTION OF X
380  Y2=Y*E/(E-Z)              ! PROJECTION OF Y
390  Z=FNG7(X2,Y2,1)           ! PLOTS POINT
400  NEXT I                    ! END OF POINT LOOP
420  PRINT CHR$(7);            ! RINGS BELL
430  SLEEP 2                   ! PAUSES WHILE FRAME IS PHOTOGRAPHED
440  Z=FNG6(1)                 ! ERASES SCREEN AND PAUSES
450  NEXT F                    ! END OF FRAME LOOP
```

After initialization of the graphics package (line 100), the program defines an internal coordinate system $(-1,-1)$ to $(+1,+1)$, which will be used in computing the positions of elements in the display (line 110). When the display is generated on the face of the cathode ray tube, the internal coordinate system will occupy scope coordinates of (150,50) to (830,730), according to line 120. A dimension statement (line 140) sets aside sufficient storage locations for the original X, Y, and Z coordinates of 100 points. The viewing distance, E, is assigned a value of 3 in the internal coordinate system (line 200). There are to be six frames in a sequence, according to line 210. The angle of rotation per frame, T, in radians, is set at $2*PI$ (i.e., 360°) divided by the number of frames, M (line 220). The number of points per frame, N, is assigned a value of 100 (line 230). Lines 240–290 generate the coordinates of the points, first randomly locating each point in a cube of side 2 (lines 250–270) and then rejecting any point that falls outside the inscribed unit radius sphere (line 280). The frames of the motion picture are produced by lines 300–450. First, the sine and cosine of the angle of rotation for the frame are determined (lines 310–320). The angle of rotation for a given frame is the product of the angle per frame, T, and the frame number, F. Then the position of each point in the display is computed and the point is plotted (lines 330–400). This is accomplished by first applying the formulas for rotation about the Y axis (lines 340–360), then applying the formulas for a polar projection of the rotated point (lines 370–380), and finally calling the plotting function in the graphics package (line 390). After all N points on frame F are plotted, the bell is sounded to trigger the camera, causing the frame to be photographed (line 420). After a two-second pause to allow the camera to operate (line 430), the screen is erased (line 440). The six frames produced by this program are shown in Figure A.2.

FIGURE A.2. Six frames produced by the sample program.

References

Ames, A. Visual perception and the rotating trapezoidal window. *Psychological Monographs*, 1951, 67 (7, Whole No. 324).

Attneave, F., & Olson, R. K. Inferences about visual mechanisms from monocular depth effects. *Psychonomic Science*, 1966, 4, 133–134.

Avant, L. L. Vision in the ganzfeld. *Psychological Bulletin*, 1965, 64, 246–258.

Baird, J. C. *Psychophysical analysis of visual space*. Oxford: Pergamon 1970.

Beck, J. Texture-gradients and judgments of slant and recession. *American Journal of Psychology*, 1960, 73, 411–416.

Berkeley, G. *An essay towards a new theory of vision*. Dublin: Jeremy Pepyat, 1709. In A.D. Lindsay (Ed.), *A new theory of vision*. London: J. M. Dent & Sons, 1957. 3-86.

Bernstein, A., Arbuckle, T., Roberts, M. deV., & Belsky, M. A. A chess playing program for the IBM 704. *Proceedings of the Western Joint Computer Conference*, 1958, 157–159.

Boring, E. G. *Sensation and perception in the history of experimental psychology*. New York: Appleton-Century-Crofts, 1942.

Boring, E. G. On the moon illusion. *Science*, 1962, 137, 902–905.

Börjesson, E. Properties of changing patterns evoking visually perceived oscillation. *Perception and Psychophysics*, 1971, 9, 303–308.

187

Börjesson, E., & von Hofsten, C. Spatial determinants of depth perception in two-dot motion patterns. *Perception and Psychophysics,* 1972, *11,* 263–268.

Börjesson, E., & von Hofsten, C. Visual perception of motion in depth: Application of a vector model to three-dot motion patterns. *Perception and Psychophysics,* 1973, *13,* 169–179.

Braunstein, M. L. Depth perception in rotating dot patterns; Effects of numerosity and perspective. *Journal of Experimental Psychology,* 1962, *64,* 415–420.

Braunstein, M. L. Sensitivity of the observer to transformations of the visual field. *Journal of Experimental Psychology,* 1966, *72,* 683–689.

Braunstein, M. L. Motion and texture as sources of slant information. *Journal of Experimental Psychology,* 1968, *78,* 247–253.

Braunstein, M. L. Perception of rotation in figures with rectangular and trapezoidal features. *Journal of Experimental Psychology,* 1971, *91,* 25–29.

Braunstein, M. L. Perception of rotation in depth: A process model. *Journal of Experimental Psychology,* 1972, *79,* 510–524.

Braunstein, M. L., & Payne, J. W. Perspective and the rotating trapezoid. *Journal of the Optical Society of America,* 1968, *58,* 399–403. (a)

Braunstein, M. L., & Payne, J. W. Slant perception in rotated grid patterns. *Proceedings of the 76th Annual Convention.* American Psychological Association, 1968, 93–94. (b)

Braunstein, M. L., & Payne, J. W. Perspective and form ratio as determinants of relative slant judgments. *Journal of Experimental Psychology,* 1969, *81,* 584–590.

Cook, T. H., Mefferd, R. B., Jr., & Wieland, B. A. Apparent reversals of orientation (perspective reversals) in depth as determinants of apparent reversals of rotary motion. *Perceptual and Motor Skills,* 1967, *24,* 691–702.

Clark, W. C., Smith, A. H., & Rabe, A. Retinal gradient of outline as a stimulus for slant. *Canadian Journal of Psychology,* 1955, *9,* 247–253.

Clark, W. C., Smith, A. H., & Rabe, A. The interaction of surface texture, outline gradient, and ground in the perception of slant. *Canadian Journal of Psychology,* 1956, *10,* 1–8. (a)

Clark, W. C., Smith, A. H., & Rabe, A. Retinal gradients of outline distortion and binocular disparity as stimuli for slant. *Canadian Journal of Psychology,* 1956, *10,* 77–81. (b)

Cross, J., & Cross, J. The misperception of rotary motion. *Perception and Psychophysics,* 1969, *5,* 94–96.

Day, R. H., & Power, R. P. Frequency of apparent reversal of rotary motion in depth as a function of shape and pattern. *Australian Journal of Psychology,* 1963, *15,* 162–174.

Day, R. H., & Power, R. P. Apparent reversal (oscillation) of rotary motion in depth: An investigation and a general theory. *Psychological Review,* 1965, *72,* 117–127.

Dees, J. W. Moon illusion and size–distance invariance: An explanation based upon an experimental artifact. *Perceptual and Motor Skills,* 1966, *23,* 629–630.

De Groot, A. D. *Thought and choice in chess.* The Hague: Mouton & Co., 1965.

Dinneen, G. P. Programming pattern recognition. *Proceedings of the 1955 Western Joint Computer Conference,* 1955, *7,* 94–100.

Duncan, F. S. Kinetic art: On my psychokinematic objects. *Leonardo,* 1975, *8,* 97–101.

Dunn, B. E., & Thomas, S. W. Relative height and relative size as monocular depth cues in the trapezoid. *Perceptual and Motor Skills,* 1966, *22,* 275–281.

Encyclopedia Britannica. Chicago: William Benton, 1968.

Epstein, W., Jansson, G., & Johansson, G. Perceived angle of oscillatory motion. *Perception and Psychophysics*, 1968, 3, 12–16.

Epstein, W., & Park, J. N. Shape constancy: Functional relationships and theoretical formulations. *Psychological Bulletin*, 1963, 60, 265–288.

Eriksson, E. S. The shape slant invariance hypothesis in static perception. *Scandinavian Journal of Psychology*, 1967, 8, 193–208.

Feigenbaum, E. A. The simulation of verbal learning behavior. *Proceedings of the Western Joint Computer Conference*, 1961, 19, 121–132.

Feldman, J. Simulation of behavior in the binary choice experiment. *Proceedings of the Western Joint Computer Conference*, 1961, 19, 133–144.

Fischer, G. J. Factors affecting estimation of depth with variations of the stereokinetic effect. *American Journal of Psychology*, 1956, 69, 252–257.

Fisichelli, V. R. Effect of rotational axis and dimensional variations on the reversals of apparent movement in Lissajous figures. *American Journal of Psychology*, 1946, 59, 669–675.

Flock, H. R. *The monocular perception of surface slant*. (Doctoral dissertation, Cornell University, 1962). Ann Arbor: University Microfilms, 1962, No. 62-2514.

Flock, H. R. A possible optical basis for monocular slant perception. *Psychological Review*, 1964, 71, 380–391. (a)

Flock, H. R. Some conditions sufficient for accurate monocular perceptions of moving surface slants. *Journal of Experimental Psychology*, 1964, 67, 560–572. (b)

Flock, H. R. Optical texture and linear perspective as stimuli for slant perception. *Psychological Review*, 1965, 72, 505–514.

Flock, H. R., & Moscatelli, A. Variables of surface texture and accuracy of space perceptions. *Perceptual and Motor Skills*, 1964, 19, 327–334.

Freeman, R. B., Jr. Ecological optics and visual slant. *Psychological Review*, 1965, 72, 501–504.

Freeman, R. B., Jr. Effect of size on visual slant. *Journal of Experimental Psychology*, 1966, 71, 96–103. (a)

Freeman, R. B., Jr. Optical texture versus retinal perspective: A reply to Flock. *Psychological Review*, 1966, 73, 365–371. (b)

Gibson, E. J., & Walk, R. D. The visual cliff. *Scientific American*, 1960, 202, 64–71.

Gibson, E. J., Gibson, J. J., Smith O. W., & Flock, H. Motion parallax as a determinant of perceived depth. *Journal of Experimental Psychology*, 1959, 58, 40–51.

Gibson, J. J. Perception of distance and space in the open air. In J. J. Gibson (Ed.), *Motion picture testing and research*. AAF program, Report #7, 1946. Reprinted in D. C. Beardslee & M. Wertheimer (Eds.), *Readings in perception*. Princeton: D. Van Nostrand, 1958.

Gibson, J. J. The perception of visual surfaces. *American Journal of Psychology*, 1950, 63, 367–384. (a)

Gibson, J. J. *The perception of the visual world*. Boston: Houghton Mifflin, 1950. (b)

Gibson, J. J. The visual perception of objective motion and subjective movement. *Psychological Review*, 1954, 61, 304–314.

Gibson, J. J. Optical motions and transformations as stimuli for visual perception. *Psychological Review*, 1957, 64, 288–295.

Gibson, J. J. *The senses considered as perceptual systems*. Boston: Houghton Mifflin, 1966.

Gibson, J. J., & Carel, W. Does motion perspective independently produce the impression of a receeding surface? *Journal of Experimental Psychology*, 1952, *44*, 16–18.

Gibson, J. J., & Gibson, E. J. Continuous perspective transformations and the perception of rigid motion. *Journal of Experimental Psychology*, 1957, *54*, 129–138.

Gillam, B. J. Perception of slant when perspective and stereopsis conflict: Experiments with aniseikonic lenses. *Journal of Experimental Psychology*, 1968, *78*, 299–305.

Gillam, B. Judgments of slant on the basis of foreshortening. *Scandinavian Journal of Psychology*, 1970, *11*, 31–34.

Gogel, W. C. The organization of perceived space: I. Perceptual interactions. *Psychologische Forschung*, 1973, *36*, 195–221. (a)

Gogel, W. C. The organization of preceived space: II. Consequences of perceptual interactions. *Psychologische Forschung*, 1973, *36*, 223–247. (b)

Graham, C. H. On some aspects of real and apparent visual movement. *Journal of the Optical Society of America*, 1963, *53*, 1019–1025.

Graham, C. H. Perception of movement. In C. H. Graham (Ed.), *Vision and visual perception*. New York: Wiley, 1965.

Graham, C. H., & Gillam, B. J. Occurrence of theoretically correct responses during rotation of the Ames window. *Perception and Psychophysics*, 1970, *8*, 257–260.

Green, B. F., Jr. Mathematical notes on 3-D rotations, 2-D perspective transformations, and dot configurations. Group Report No. 58-5, Massachusetts Institute of Technology, Lincoln Laboratory, 1959.

Green, B. F., Jr. Figure coherence in the kinetic depth effect. *Journal of Experimental Psychology*, 1961, *62*, 272–282.

Gregory, R. L. Human perception. *British Medical Bulletin*, 1964, *20*, 21–26.

Gregory, R. L. *The intelligent eye*. New York: McGraw-Hill, 1970.

Gruber, H. E., & Clark, W. C. Perception of slanted surfaces. *Perceptual and Motor Skills*, 1956, *6*, 97–106.

Hay, J. C. Optical motions and space perception: An extension of Gibson's analysis. *Psychological Review*, 1966, *73*, 550–565.

Hershberger, W. A. Comment on "Apparent reversal (oscillation) of rotary motion in depth." *Psychological Review*, 1967, *74*, 235–238.

Hershberger, W. A., & Carpenter, D. L. Veridical rotation in depth in unidimensional polar projections devoid of three motion-parallax cues. *Journal of Experimental Psychology*, 1972, *93*, 213–216.

Hershberger, W. A., Carpenter, D. L., Starzec, J., & Laughlin, N. K. Simulation of an object rotating in depth: Constant and reversed projection ratios. *Journal of Experimental Psychology*, 1974, *103*, 844–853.

Hershberger, W. A., & Starzec, J. J. Motion-parallax cues in one-dimensional polar and parallel projections: Differential velocity and acceleration/displacement change. *Journal of Experimental Psychology*, 1974, *103*, 717–723.

Hershberger, W. A., & Urban, D. Depth perception from motion parallax in one-dimensional polar projections: Projection versus viewing distance. *Journal of Experimental Psychology*, 1970, *86*, 157–164. (a)

Hershberger, W. A., & Urban, D. Three motion-parallax cues in one-dimensional polar projections of rotation in depth. *Journal of Experimental Psychology*, 1970, *86*, 380–383. (b)

Jansson, G., & Börjesson, E. Perceived direction of rotary motion. *Perception and Psychophysics*, 1969, *6*, 19–26.

Johansson, G. *Configurations in event perception*. Uppsala: Almqvist & Wiksell, 1950.

Johansson, G. Perception of motion and changing form. *Scandinavian Journal of Psychology*, 1964, 5, 181–208.

Johansson, G. On theories for visual space perception: A letter to Gibson. *Scandinavian Journal of Psychology*, 1970, 11, 67–74.

Johansson, G. Visual perception of rotary motion as transformations of conic sections. *Psychologia*, 1974, 17, 226–237.

Johansson, G., & Jansson, G. *A model for space perception and object perception from changes in a straight line*. (Report No. 41). Uppsala, Sweden: University of Uppsala, Department of Psychology, 1967.

Johansson, G., & Jansson, G. Perceived rotary motion from changes in a straight line. *Perception and Psychophysics*, 1968, 6, 193–198.

Julesz, B. Binocular depth perception of computer-generated patterns. *Bell System Technical Journal*, 1960, 39, 1125–1162.

Julesz, B. *Foundations of cyclopean perception*. Chicago: University of Chicago Press, 1971.

Kahneman, D., & Tversky, A. Subjective probability: A judgment of representativeness. *Cognitive Psychology*, 1972, 3, 430–454.

Kahneman, D., & Tversky, A. On the psychology of prediction. *Psychological Review*, 1973, 80, 237–251.

Kenyon, F. C. A curious optical illusion connected with an electric fan. *Science*, 1898, 8, 371–372.

Kepler, J. Ad vitellionem paralipomena, quibus astronomiae pars optica traditur. Frankfurt, 1604. (Trans. by A. C. Crombie.) In R. J. Hernstein & E. G. Boring, (Eds.), *A source book in the history of psychology*. Cambridge: Harvard University Press, 1966.

Key, W. B. *Subliminal seduction*. Englewood Cliffs, N.J.: Prentice Hall, 1973.

Kilpatrick, F. P. (Ed.) *Human behavior from the transactional point of view*. Hanover, N.H.: Institute for Associated Research, 1952.

Kilpatrick, F. P., & Ittelson, W. H. Three demonstrations involving the perception of movement. *Journal of Experimental Psychology*, 1951, 42, 394–402.

Koffka, K. *Principles of gestalt psychology*. New York: Harcourt, 1935.

Leibowitz, H. W. *Visual perception*. New York: Macmillan, 1965.

Lichtenstein, S., & Slovic, P. Reversals of preference between bids and choices in gambling decisions. *Journal of Experimental Psychology*, 1971, 89, 46–55.

Lichtenstein, S., Slovic, P., & Zinc, D. Effect of instruction in expected value on optimality of gambling decisions. *Journal of Experimental Psychology*, 1969, 79, 236–240.

Locke, J. *An essay concerning human understanding* (Vol. 1). In A. C. Fraser, Ed., 3rd ed., 1694. Oxford: Clarendon, 1894. (Reprinted, New York: Dover, 1959)

Maloney, R. Inflexible logic. *The New Yorker*, 1940. Reprinted in J. R. Newman (Ed.), *The world of mathematics*. (Vol. 4). New York: Simon and Schuster, 1956.

Mefferd, R. B., Jr., & Weiland, B. A. Perception of depth in rotating objects: 2. Perspective as a determinant of stereokinesis. *Perceptual and Motor Skills*, 1967, 25, 621–628.

Metzger, W. *Gesetze der Sehens*, Frankfurt am Main: Waldemar Kramer, 1953.

Mikaelian, H., & Held, R. Two types of adaptation to an optically rotated visual field. *American Journal of Psychology*, 1964, 77, 257–263.

Miles, W. Figure for the windmill illusion. *Journal of General Psychology*, 1929, 2, 143–145.

Miles, W. R. Movement interpretations of the silhouette of a revolving fan. *American Journal of Psychology*, 1931, *43*, 392–405.

Miller, G. A. The magical number seven, plus or minus two. *Psychological Review*, 1956, *63*, 81–97.

Minsky, M. A framework for representing knowledge. In P. H. Winston (Ed.), *The psychology of computer vision*. New York: McGraw-Hill, 1975.

Molyneux, W. *Dioptrica nova: A treatise of dioptrics*. London, 1692. Reprinted in R. J. Herrnstein & E. G. Boring (Eds.), *A source book in the history of psychology*. Cambridge: Harvard University Press, 1966.

Murch, G. M. The perception of rotary motion. *Journal of Experimental Psychology*, 1970, *86,* 83–85.

Musatti, C. L. Sui fenomeni stereocinetici. *Archivio Italiano di Psicologia*, 1924, *3*, 105–120.

Musatti, C. L. Forma e assimilazione. *Archivio Italiano di Psicologia*. 1931, *9*, 61–156.

Newell, A., Shaw, J. C., & Simon, H. A. Chess-playing programs and the problem of complexity. *IBM Journal of Research and Development*, 1958, *2*, 320–335.

Newell, A., & Simon, H. A. *Human problem solving*. Englewood Cliffs, N.J.: Prentice Hall, 1972.

Ogle, K. N. *Researches in binocular vision*. New York: Hafner, 1950.

Osgood, C. E. *Method and theory in experimental psychology*. New York: Oxford, 1953.

Pastore, N. Some remarks on the Ames oscillatory effect. *Psychological Review*, 1952, *59*, 319–323.

Pastore, N. *Selective history of theories of visual perception: 1650–1950*. New York: Oxford, 1971.

Payne, J. W. Alternative approaches to decision making under risk: Moments versus risk dimensions. *Psychological Bulletin*, 1973, *80*, 439–453.

Payne, J. W., & Braunstein, M. L. Preferences among gambles with equal underlying distributions. *Journal of Experimental Psychology*, 1971, *87*, 13–18.

Philip, B. R., & Fisichelli, V. R. Effect of speed of rotation and complexity of pattern on the reversals of apparent movement in Lissajous figures. *American Journal of Psychology*, 1945, *58*, 530–539.

Phillips, R. J. Stationary visual texture and the estimation of slant angle. *Quarterly Journal of Experimental Psychology*, 1970, *22*, 389–397.

Polya, G. *How to solve it*. Princeton: Princeton University Press, 1945.

Porta, J. B. *Natural magic*. Naples: 1589. Trans. 1658. New York: Basic Books, 1957.

Power, R. P. Stimulus properties which reduce apparent reversal of rotating rectangular shapes. *Journal of Experimental Psychology*, 1967, *73*, 595–599.

Power, R. P., & Day, R. H. Constancy and illusion of apparent direction of rotary motion in depth: Tests of a theory. *Perception & Psychophysics*, 1973, *13*, 217–223.

Reddy, R., Rosen, B., Kriz, S., Powell, M., & Broadley, B. Computer graphics in research: Some state-of-the-art systems. *American Psychologist*, 1975, *30*, 239–246.

Reed, S. K. *Psychological processes in pattern recognition*. New York: Academic Press, 1973.

Richter, I. A. (Ed.) *Selections from the notebooks of Leonardo Da Vinci*. London: Oxford, 1952.

Rock, I. Adaptation to a minified image. *Psychonomic Science*, 1965, *2*, 105–106.

Rock, I., & Kaufman, L. The moon illusion: II. *Science*, 1962, *136*, 1023–1031.

Schwarz, A. *The complete works of Marcel Duchamp*. London: Thames and Hudson, 1969.

Selfridge, O. F. Pattern recognition and modern computers. *Proceedings of the 1955 Joint Computer Conference,* 1955, 7, 91–93.

Selfridge, O. G., & Neisser, U. Pattern recognition by machine. *Scientific American,* 1960, 203, 60–68.

Simon, H. A., & Newell, A. Human problem solving: The state of the theory in 1970. *American Psychologist,* 1971, 26, 145–159.

Skavenski, A. A., & Steinman, R. M. Control of eye position in the dark. *Vision Research,* 1970, 10, 193–203.

Slovic, P. *From Shakespeare to Simon: Speculations—and some evidence—about man's ability to process information* (ORI Research Bulletin, 12, No. 2). Eugene, Ore.: Oregon Research Institute, April 1972.

Smith, A. H. Judgment of slant with constant outline convergence and variable surface texture gradient. *Perceptual and Motor Skills,* 1964, 18, 869–875.

Smith, A. H. Perceived slant as a function of stimulus contour and vertical dimension. *Perceptual and Motor Skills,* 1967, 24, 167–173.

Smith, O. W., & Gruber, H. Perception of depth in photographs. *Perceptual and Motor Skills,* 1958, 8, 307–313.

Stavrianos, B. K. The relation of shape perception to explicit judgments of inclination. *Archives of Psychology,* 1945, No. 296.

Stratton, G. M. Some preliminary experiments on vision without inversion of the retinal image. *Psychological Review,* 1896, 3, 611–617.

Stratton, G. M. Upright vision and the retinal image. *Psychological Review,* 1897, 4, 182–187. (a)

Stratton, G. M. Vision without inversion of the retinal image. *Psychological Review,* 1897, 4, 341–360; 463–481. (b)

Tichomirov, O. K., & Poznyanskaya, E. D. An investigation of visual search as a means of analyzing heuristics. *Soviet Psychology,* 1966, 5, 2-15. [Translated from *Voropsy Psikhologii,* 1966, 12, 39–53.]

Tversky, A., & Kahneman, D. Availability: A heuristic for judging frequency and probability. *Cognitive Psychology,* 1973, 5, 207–232.

Tversky, A., & Kahneman, D. Judgment under uncertainty: Heuristics and biases. *Science,* 1974, 185, 1124–1131.

Uhr, L., & Vossler, C. Suggestions for a general purpose adaptive computer model of brain functions. *Behavioral Science,* 1961, 5, 91–97.

Voltaire, F. M. A. *The elements of Sir Isaac Newton's Philosophy.* London, 1738. (Trans. by John Hanna.) London: Cass, 1967.

Wallach, H., & Karsh, E. B. The modification of stereoscopic depth-perception and the kinetic depth effect. *American Journal of Psychology,* 1963, 76, 429–435.

Wallach, H., & O'Connell, D. N. The kinetic depth effect. *Journal of Experimental Psychology,* 1953, 45, 205–217.

Wallach, H., O'Connell, N., & Neisser, U. The memory effect of visual perception of three-dimensional form. *Journal of Experimental Psychology,* 1953, 45, 360–368.

Wallach, H., Weisz, A., & Adams, P. A. Circles and derived figures in rotation. *American Journal of Psychology,* 1956, 69, 48–59.

Weber, C. O. Apparent movement in Lissajous figures. *American Journal of Psychology,* 1930, 42, 647–649.

Wheatstone, C. Contributions to the physiology of vision. —Part the first. On some remarkable and hitherto unobserved, phenomena of binocular vision. *Philosophical Transactions of the Royal Society of London,* 1838, 128, 371–394.

White, B. J., & Mueser, G. E. Accuracy in reconstructing the arrangement of elements generating kinetic depth displays. *Journal of Experimental Psychology*, 1960, 60, 1–11.

Winston, P. H. (Ed.). *The psychology of computer vision*. New York: McGraw-Hill, 1975.

Woodworth, R. S., & Schlosberg, H. *Experimental psychology*. New York: Henry Holt and Company, 1954.

Zegers, R. T. The reversal illusion of the Ames trapezoid. *Transactions of the New York Academy of Sciences*, 1964, 26, 377–400.

Index

195

A 6
B 7
C 8
D 9
E 0
F 1
G 2
H 3
I 4
J 5